LESSONS OF THE MASTERS

THE
CHARLES ELIOT NORTON
LECTURES

2001–2002

LESSONS OF
THE MASTERS

◇ ◇ ◇

GEORGE STEINER

HARVARD UNIVERSITY PRESS
CAMBRIDGE, MASSACHUSETTS
LONDON, ENGLAND
2003

Library of Congress Cataloging-in-Publication Data

Steiner, George, 1929–
Lessons of the masters / George Steiner.
p. cm.—(The Charles Eliot Norton lectures; 2001–2002)
Includes index.
ISBN 0-674-01207-0 (alk. paper)
1. College teaching—Philosophy.
2. Teacher-student relationships.
I. Title.   II. Series

LB2331.S74 2003
378.1'2—dc21   2003047800

For Rebecca, for Miriam, one day.

ACKNOWLEDGEMENTS

◇   ◇   ◇

HEARTFELT THANKS are due to Harvard University for inviting me to give these Charles Eliot Norton Lectures for 2001–02.

During my stay the courtesy, the warmth of welcome in the English Department were unfailing. As was the spirited support of stellar members of the Afro-American Studies programme.

William Logan, poet and critic, contributed invaluable touches of Americana.

My son, Professor David Steiner of Boston University, and his wife, Dr. Evelyne Ender (my sometime student), will know what their presence meant to me.

Throughout, the companionship in teaching and in study of my wife, Dr. Zara Steiner, has been exemplary.

GS
Cambridge (UK)
October 2002

CONTENTS

◇   ◇   ◇

INTRODUCTION

◇   ◇   ◇

HAVING TAUGHT for half a century, and in numerous countries and systems of higher education, I have found myself increasingly uncertain as to the legitimacy, as to the underlying truths of this "profession." I put that word in quotes to signal its complex roots in religious and ideological antecedents. The profession of the "professor," itself a somewhat opaque term, spans every conceivable nuance from making a routine, disenchanted living to an exalted sense of vocation. It comprises numerous typologies ranging from that of the soul-destroying pedagogue to that of the charismatic Master. Immersed as we are in almost innumerable forms of teaching—elementary, technical, scientific, humanistic, moral, and philosophic—we rarely step back to consider the wonders of transmission, the resources of falsehood, what I would call, pending more precise and material definition, the *mystery* of the thing. What empowers a man or a woman to teach another human being, where lies the wellspring of authority?

In turn, what are some of the main orders of response by those taught? The question vexed St. Augustine and has become raw in the libertarian climate of our own day.

Simplifying, one makes out three principal scenarios or structures of relation. Masters have destroyed their disciples both psychologically and, in rarer cases, physically. They have broken their spirits, consumed their hopes, exploited their dependence and individuality. The domain of the soul has its vampires. In counterpoint, disciples, pupils, apprentices have subverted, betrayed, and ruined their Masters. Again, this drama has both mental and physical attributes. Newly elected Rector, the triumphant Wagner will spurn the dying Faust, his sometime *magister*. The third category is that of exchange, of an eros of reciprocal trust and, indeed, love ("the loving disciple" at the Last Supper). By a process of interaction, of osmosis, the Master learns from his disciple as he teaches him. The intensity of the dialogue generates friendship in the highest sense. It can enlist both the clear-sightedness and unreason of love. Consider Alcibiades and Socrates, Heloise and Abelard, Arendt and Heidegger. There are disciples who have felt unable to survive their Masters.

Each of these modes of relation, and the boundless possibilities of mixture and nuance between them, have inspired religious, philosophic, literary, sociological, and scientific witness. The material defies any comprehensive survey, being truly planetary. The chapters that follow seek to provide the most summary of introductions; they are almost absurdly selective.

At issue will be questions both rooted in historical circumstance and perennial. The axes of time cross and recross. What does it mean to transmit (*tradendere*) and from whom to whom is such transmission legitimate? The relations between *traditio,* "what has been handed down," and what the Greeks called *paradidomena,* "that which is being handed down *now,*" are never transparent. It may be no accident that the semantics of "treason" and "traduction" are not altogether removed from those of "tradition." In turn, these vibrations of sense and of intention are strongly operative in the concept, itself constantly challenging, of "translation" (*translatio*). Is teaching, in some fundamental sense, a mode of translation, an exercise between the lines as Walter Benjamin would have it when he assigns eminent virtues of fidelity and transfer to the interlinear? We will see that many answers are on offer.

Genuine teaching has been held to be an *imitatio* of a transcendent or, more precisely divine, act of disclosure, of that unfolding and folding inward of truths which Heidegger attributes to Being (*aletheia*). The secular primer or advanced study are mimetic of a sacred, canonic template and original which was itself, in philosophic and mythological readings, communicated orally. The teacher is no more, but also no less, than an auditor and messenger whose inspired, then schooled, receptivity has enabled him to apprehend a revealed *Logos,* that "Word in the beginning." This is, in essence, the validating model of the teacher of Torah, of the explicator of the Koran, of the commentator on the New Testament. By analogy—and how many perplexities surface in the uses of the analogous—this paradigm extends to the imparting, to the transmission and codification of secular knowledge, of *sapientia* or *Wissenschaft.* Already in the Masters of holy writ and its exegesis we find ideals and practises which will modulate into the secular sphere. Thus St. Augustine, Akiba, and Thomas Aquinas belong to any history of pedagogy.

In contrast, it has been argued that the only honest, verifiable license for teaching, for didactic authority, is by virtue of example. The teacher demonstrates to the student his own grasp of the material, his ability to perform the chemical experiment (the laboratory houses "demonstrators"), his capacity to solve the equation on the blackboard, to draw accurately the plaster cast or living nude in the atelier. Exemplary teaching is enactment and can be mute. Perhaps it ought to be. The hand guides that of the pupil on the piano keys. Valid teaching is ostensible. It shows. This "ostentation," so intriguing to Wittgenstein, is embedded in etymology: Latin *dicere* "to show" and, only later, "to show by saying"; Middle English *token* and *techen* with its implicit connotations of "that which shows." (Is the teacher, finally, a showman?) In German, *deuten* signifying to "point to" is inseparable from *bedeuten,* "to mean." The contiguity compels Wittgenstein to deny the possibility of any honest textual instruction in philosophy. In regard to morality, only the actual life of the Master has demonstrative proof. Socrates and saints teach by existing.

Both these scenarios may be idealizations. Simplified though it be, Foucault's perspective has its pertinence. Teaching could be regarded as an exercise, open or concealed, in power relations. The Master possesses psychological, social, physical power. He can reward and punish, exclude and promote. His authority is institutional or charismatic or both. It is sustained by promise or menace. Knowledge, praxis themselves, as defined and transmitted by a pedagogic system, by the instruments of schooling, are forms of power. In that sense, even the more radical modes of instruction are conservative and charged with the ideological values of stability (in French, "tenure" is *stabilization*). Today's "countercultures" and New Age polemics, with their ancestry in the quarrel with books found in religious primitivism and pastoral anarchy, brand formal knowledge and scientific research as strategies of exploitation, of class dominance. Who teaches what to whom and towards what political ends? It is, as we will see, this scheme of mastery, of teaching as brute power, raised to the pitch of erotic hysteria, which is satirized in Eugène Ionesco's *La Leçon.*

Virtually unexamined, are refusals to teach, denials of transmission. The Master finds no disciples, no receivers worthy of his message, of his inheritance. Moses destroys the first set of Tables, precisely those written in God's own hand. Nietzsche is obsessed by the lack of adequate disciples just when his need for reception is agonizing. This motif is Zarathustra's tragedy.

Or it may be that the *doxa,* the doctrine and material to be taught, are judged too dangerous to be handed on. They are buried in some secret place, not to be rediscovered for a long time or, more drastically, allowed to die with the Master. There are examples in the history of alchemical and Kabbalistic lore. More often, only a handful of the elect, of the initiate, will receive the Master's true meaning. The public at large is fed a diluted, vulgarized version. This distinction between esoteric and exoteric versions animates Leo Strauss's readings of Plato. Are there today possible parallels in biogenetics or particle physics? Are there hypotheses too threatening (socially, humanly) to be tested, and discoveries to be left unpublished? Military secrets might be the farcical guise of a more complex and clandestine dilemma.

There can also be loss, disappearance via accident, via self-deception—had Fermat solved his own theorem?—or historical action. How much oral wisdom and science, in botany and therapy for example, has been irretrievably lost, how many manuscripts and books have been burned, from Alexandria to Sarajevo? Only suspect shreds survive of the Albigensian scriptures. It is a haunting possibility that certain "truths," that certain seminal metaphors and insights, notably in the humanities, have been lost, destroyed irrevocably (Aristotle on comedy). We are, today, unable to reproduce, except photographically, certain tints mixed by Van Eyck. Reportedly, we cannot perform certain triple-stopped *fermata* which Paganini refused to teach. By what means were those cyclopean stones transported to Stonehenge or made upright on Easter Island?

Obviously, the arts and acts of teaching are, in the proper sense of that abused term, dialectical. The Master learns from the disciple and is modified by this interrelation in what becomes, ideally, a process of exchange. Donation becomes reciprocal, as in the labyrinths of love. "I am most I when I am you" as Paul Celan put it. Masters repudiate disciples finding them unworthy or disloyal. The disciple, in turn, feels that he has outgrown his Master, that he must relinquish his Master in order to become himself (Wittgenstein will enjoin him to do so). This overcoming of the Master, with its psychoanalytic components of Oedipal rebellion, can cause traumatic sorrow. As in Dante's farewell to Virgil in the *Purgatorio* or in Kawabata's *Master of Go.* Or it may be a source of vindictive satisfaction both in fiction—Wagner triumphs over Faust— and fact—Heidegger prevails over and humbles Husserl.

It is some of these manifold encounters in philosophy, in literature, in music, I now want to look at.

1

LASTING ORIGINS

◇ ◇ ◇

INSTRUCTION, spoken and enacted, by word or exemplary demonstration, is obviously as ancient as mankind. There can be no family or social system, however isolated and rudimentary, without teaching and pupillage, without achieved mastery and apprenticeship. But the western legacy has its specific sources. To a striking degree, the usages, the motifs which continue to implement our schooling, our pedagogic conventions, our image of the Master and his disciples, together with the rivalries among competing schools or doctrines, have preserved their lineaments since the sixth century B.C. The spirit of our lectures and seminars, the charismatic claims of rival gurus and their acolytes, many of the rhetorical techniques of teaching itself, would not surprise the pre-Socratics. It is this millennial continuity which may be our principal inheritance and the axis of what we call, always provisionally, western culture.

The trouble is that we know too much and too little of

such figures as Empedocles, Heraclitus, Pythagoras, or Parmenides. Their purported lives have never ceased to fascinate philosophic and poetic sensibility. They quicken not only cosmological, metaphysical, and logical argument throughout western intellectual history, but art, poetry, and, in the case of Pythagoras, conceptions of music. Yet their actual teachings have come down to us, if at all, in fragments, in torn shreds as it were or via the citations, themselves possibly inaccurate and even opportunistic, of such critical voices as those of Plato, of Aristotle, of Byzantine doxographers and the Church Fathers. A mist of legend, although often strangely luminous, surrounds the philosophic-scientific teachings and methods of pre-Socratic Sicily and Asia Minor. Even the rubric "philosophic-scientific" is questionable. The pre-Socratics do not make this distinction. Elements of allegory, of esoteric cults, of magic as we know it from Shamanic practices are inextricably inwoven with propositions of an arduously abstract tenor (Parmenides on "nothingness," Heraclitus on the dialectic). Hegel's image is arresting: it is only with Heraclitus that the history of philosophy, which is itself philosophy, reaches dry land. Heraclitus, the dark and riddling aphorist, as the ancients designated him, is, however, as elusive as his twilit predecessors.

And at once, we come upon one of our major themes: that of orality. Before writing, during the history of writing and in challenge to it, the spoken word is integral to the act of teaching. The Master *speaks* to the disciple. From Plato to Wittgenstein, the ideal of lived truth is one of orality, of face-to-face address and response. To many eminent teachers and thinkers, the setting down of their lessons in the mute immobility of a script is an inevitable falsification and betrayal.

To Heidegger, Anaximander was an immediate presence. But already to classical antiquity such primal Masters, often itinerant, as Anaximander, Anaxagoras, Xenophanes, and Ion of Chios were something of a mystery. How and whom had they taught, what exactly was meant by early references to a "school" of Anaxagoras? Legend and conjecture inclined to relate "Orphism," the teachings and rites which mythography ascribed to the figure of Orpheus, to the dawn of philosophical-cosmological instruction. Orphism remains an almost impenetrable concept and tradition. What is significant are the intimate affinities between philosophic pedagogy on the one hand and the arts of the rhapsode on the other. These arts are oral and, by definition, poetic. The recitation of rhapsodes, of more or less necromantic poet-singers, the treatises of Masters themselves presented in poetic forms (Empedocles, Parmenides but also Platonic mythology), the establishment of initiate communities of adepts and disciples made for a now unrecapturable but seminal brew. Its force can be gauged from the traces it has left in modern practise.

It is in what we know of the teachings and hagiographic narratives which surround Empedocles and Pythagoras that the overarching themes of Mastery and discipleship originate. By the later fifth century, Pythagoras's renown and the enactments of his precepts were widespread. Considered a universal man (Heraclitus will denounce this polymath "charlatanry"), Pythagoras exercised a commanding influence over cosmography, mathematics, the understanding of music and, above all, the conduct of daily lives of an ascetic, purified character. The spell which radiated from his teaching in Crotona must have been mesmeric. In his study of the pre-Socratics, a sceptical Jonathan Barnes tells of "numerous sectarians," of a Pythagorean "Freemasonry—united by pre-scriptions and taboos—a religious society, not a scientific guild, which dabbled in South Italian politics."

It is this "dabbling" which may have proved fatal. It would appear that Pythagoras gathered around him a coven drawn from the local aristocracy. Tenacious legend evokes years of preparation, of initiatory silences, of strict dietary and hy-gienic observance before members of this grouping (*etaireia*) were admitted to the Master's presence and personal teach-ing. Though ethical and intellectual commitments were un-doubtedly paramount, Pythagoras's vision and doctrines had political implications. They aimed at nothing less than the rule of philosophy over the city—the Platonic ideal. The tra-dition whereby the citizenry rose against Pythagoras compel-ling him to flee to Metapontum in c. 497–5 B.C. is not im-plausible. There, reports not untainted by mysticism, have it that the Master passed away after abstaining from nourish-ment for forty days (those "forty days in the desert"?).

But discipleship did not cease. Pythagorean communities seem to have persisted in cities under Crotona's influence. At-tacked in c. 450, later Pythagoreans fled to Greece. "Bound in fellowship by custom and ritual," they can be traced down to c. 340 B.C. A recurrent pattern of conflict between the life of the mind and that of the city had begun. Also Orpheus had been torn to pieces and Hebraic intuition will insist that prophets and teachers of wisdom are slain by their fellow citi-zens.

This conflict features in what we know of Empedocles. Here the aura of the supernatural is even more pronounced than in respect of Pythagoras. Empedocles surrounds his au-gust, inspired person with *hetairoi,* pupils, companions, women among them. His didactic practices with their Orphic-Pythagorean or Parmenidian precedent point to a fundamental orality, though in this instance a philosophic-poetic text has come down to us. The issue of political ambition is unmistakable. Empedocles's philosophical-magical *doxa,* whose inner and esoteric precepts are offered only to a chosen elite, entails the possibility of political rule over Syracuse or Agrigento. The motif whereby Empedocles refuses the crown urged upon him by the people is an ancient one. As is the tradition whereby he exercised some form of despotic rule, including the execution of his enemies. Hence, according to one biographical tradition, a popular uprising and the sage's banishment to the Peloponnesus. The other version will become immensely celebrated. Shattered by the hatred of the priestly caste and the mob, bidding farewell to Pausanias, his elect disciple who will become an eminent physician, Empedocles ascends the lone wilderness of Mount Etna and leaps into its fiery crater. A sandal, found on the glowing rim, tells of his suicide.

Yet his doctrinal, stylistic influence carries on. An Empedoclean school of medicine flourishes in Syracuse in the fourth century B.C. As late as the sixth century A.D., the Neoplatonist Simplicius reads Empedocles in the format of a scroll. Above all, it is the high drama of Empedocles's legendary death, and of its philosophic-social implications which will continue to exercise their fascination. We will turn later to Friedrich Hölderlin's *Tod des Empedokles* in its threefold versions. Novalis projects an Empedocles drama. So does Nietzsche when he plans a tragedy in prose. Only one scene survives, but the material is rich with self-portrayal. Nietzsche's Empedocles will turn knowledge against himself; he wills the ruin of his people because their sloth and mediocrity are incurable. He "hardens himself more and more." These themes, and the "Empedocles landscape," are closely reflected in *Thus Spake Zarathustra*. Indeed, the *imago* of the Master's ascent and death in the high places becomes archetypal. It inspires Ibsen and provides a telling contrast to Socrates's urbanity. Gerhart Hauptmann's "Indiphodi" dramatizes the volcanic suicide. Other poets and dramatists dwell on Empedocles's erotic relations with one or more of his entranced pupils.

Matthew Arnold's *Empedocles on Etna* is an interminable, leaden exercise. But it contains an important pointer. Broils "tear us in twain, since this new swarm / Of sophists has got empire in our schools." The "sophist brood hath overlaid / The last spark of man's consciousness with words." Who, then, were these destructive sophists?

The name has been pejorative throughout our history. It connotes mendacious argument, the ability to take either side of a case with equal and factitious rhetorical brio, logical virtuosity without substance or moral reference. Sophistry designates verbal ostentation and the self-serving play of rehearsed eloquence. It is only in recent decades that this traditional and proverbial indictment has been reconsidered, that the two major schools of sophistry in the ancient world—first Greek, then Roman—have been revalued. The revision proposed is nothing less than revolutionary. The principal Sophists and their disciples are now seen as begetters of textual criticism (cf. Protagoras's explication of a lyric by Simonides). Their audacious speculations on "nothingness," on the paradoxical status of existential propositions, notably by Gorgias, are held to contain *in nuce* Heidegger's experience of the

Nichts and consequential aspects of Lacanian-Derridean deconstructive wordplay. Isocrates, Alcidamas, then Hippias of Elis seem to share a fascination with language, with "grammatology" which radically anticipates on our most recent philosophic-semiotic interests. So eminent a scholar as Jacqueline de Romilly perceives in the Sophists indispensable agents of what we call Athenian democracy.

Most pertinent to my context is their role in the development of teaching, of the academic and the book world as we know them. The Sophists read out to their students, in what we can justly envision as lectures and seminars, both the classical authors whom they were expounding and their own writings (*paradeigmata*). If the tradition whereby Protagoras's works were burnt on grounds of atheism (416–415 B.C.?) is reliable, it provides evidence of the dissemination of written scrolls and of their sale to private owners. Polemic evidence is contained as well in the Socratic-Platonic critiques of sophistic bookishness, of the Sophists' reliance on the inert authority of the script, in *Protagoras,* in *Phaedrus,* in Plato's *Letters* II and VII. Somehow, the Sophists were able to overcome what Rudolf Pfeiffer has termed "the deep-rooted Greek aversion for the written word." Our conventions of systematic pedagogy, of hermeneutic and grammatical analysis, of textual citation are put in place. Techniques are evolved to train the student (*paideuein*) in rigorous thought and attention to detail. These are intended to form the basis, technical and thus teachable, for rhetoric and rhetorical skills. For despite their cultivated literacy and "modernity," the Sophists claimed the divinely inspired rhapsodes, the singers of truth as their predecessors.

Each of these elements is mirrored in Socrates, whose

stance towards Protagoras and Gorgias is a very complicated hybrid of irony and respect, of rebuttal and *mimesis.* To contemporaries, Socrates was himself an eminent Sophist. His arguments are not always superior to those of his adversarial kindred (notably in *Protagoras*). His sense of similitude betrays itself and, at certain points, disturbs him. Insight into this ambiguity fuels Aristophanes's mockery in *Clouds.*

Aristophanes's satire touches on a vital if intractable concern (strangely, Leo Strauss all but elides it in his *Socrates and Aristophanes*). Proceeding from town to town, lecturing in private houses and public spaces, the Sophists ask for and receive payment. It is reported that Prodicus charges fifty drachmae—a considerable sum—for his lessons on the proper usage of words and syntax.

The philosophic, moral, and epistemological implications are nothing short of boundless. They engage every aspect of our theme. How is it possible to *pay* for the transmission of wisdom, of knowledge, of ethical doctrine or logical insights? What monetary equivalence or rate of exchange can be calculated as between human sagacity and the bestowal of truth on the one hand and an honorarium in cash on the other? If the Master is truly a bearer and communicator of life-enhancing truths, a being inspired by vision and vocation of no ordinary sort, how is it possible for him to present a bill? Is there not something at once demeaning and risible about the entire situation (cf. *Clouds,* ll. 658ff., or Rabelais on the Sorbonne)?

Nuances, discriminations are, to be sure, necessary. Technical skills, the teaching of crafts, even, perhaps, of the higher reaches of technology as these impinge on the sciences, may have their fiscal rationale. The motions of carpentry and those of electronic or quantum computation do not only modulate palpably into the "professional"; the time and operative disciplines involved in them can reasonably be held to be calculable and susceptible of monetary reward. It may well be, though in a simplified sense, that the distinction to be argued is that between the teaching of applied mathematics and pure mathematics, between the geometries required by the surveyor or hydraulic engineer and the addictions of the number theorist (the borderline being always contingent and open to revision). Music affords a peculiarly challenging problem. Is there any partition possible between, say, the training of a voice, the teaching of counterpoint and that of composition itself? Or is music, even at its loftiest, a *technē* whose values can, in the last analyses, be matched and reimbursed monetarily?

But what of philosophic, ethical, cognitive material, what of poetics? The rhapsode, Plato's omniscient Ion, the Orpheus who sings for the Argonauts can be fairly rewarded for his *performance,* for that which in ancient times often associates his art with that of the prize-winning athlete. But how can we evaluate and pay for Parmenides on "the one," Socrates on virtue, Kant on the synthetic *a priori?* Do inadequately paid metaphysicians go on strike, do they withhold their labour from those unable to pay for their *magisterium?* Do differing price tags attach, say, to Heidegger's ontology and the merry liberalities and relativism of Richard Rorty? This absolutely fundamental query is masked by the fact of the academic. Because, precisely since the Sophists, so very much of philosophy "gets done" in universities and by men and women with public, professional qualifications, just because the participants in this enterprise expect and receive salaries, we tend to overlook the problematic strangeness of their trade. Because so many of the Masters from Aristotle to Bergson or Quine have been "professors," titled members of a mandarin guild, with its mechanics of appointment, promotion and financial reward, the condition seems "normal." There have been impressive dissenters, men or women whom private income dispensed from the academy: Schopenhauer and Nietzsche, for example. There have been thinkers of the stature of Sartre who found academic pedagogy unacceptable and earned their livelihood "outside." Wittgenstein occupied a university chair, though he regarded this condition as radically false. Today, the "poet in residence," the teacher of "creative writing" may be regarded, may consider himself as in a false situation. And Freud himself betrayed unease at the code of monetary remuneration for the offer of therapeutic perception. The abstentions of Spinoza have lost nothing of their exemplary radiance.

To ask whether teachers of philosophy, of literature, and poetics—what the Sophists called "rhetoric"—should expect and accept payment is to tread on unnerving ground. It is to invite, from a university audience, many of whose younger members are under more or less severe economic stress, a charge of provocative sophistry (here, the pejorative usage is exactly right). But the issue is genuine.

Authentic teaching is a vocation. It is a calling. The wealth, the exactions of meaning which relate to such terms as "ministry," "clerisy," "priesthood" modulate into secular teaching both morally and historically. Hebrew *rabbi* simply signifies "teacher." But it reminds us of an immemorial dignity. At its most elementary levels—which are, in fact, never "elementary"—in the teaching, for example, of young children, of the deaf-mute, of the mentally impaired, or at the pinnacles of privilege, in the high places of the arts, of science, of thought, authentic teaching results from a summons. "Why are you calling me, what would you have me do?" asks the prophet of the voice which calls to him or asks the rationalist of his own conscience. Ovid's understanding of Pythagoras in *Metamorphoses* XV remains talismanic:

> His thought
> Reached far aloft, to the great gods in Heaven,
> And his imagination looked on visions
> Beyond his mortal sight. All things he studied
> With watchful eager mind, and he brought home
> What he had learned and sat among the people
> Teaching them what was worthy, and they listened
> In silence . . .

The teacher is aware of the magnitude and, if you will, mystery of his profession, of that which he has professed in an unspoken Hippocratic oath. He has taken vows. There are affinities, always to be questioned, even ironized, to the oracular: *sequar or moventem / Rite deum Delphosque meos ipsumque recludam* ("I will now follow the god to the open Delphi which I carry within myself").

> There is no greater wonder than to range
> The starry heights, to leave the earth's dull regions,
> To ride the clouds, to stand on Atlas' shoulders,
> And see far off, far down, the little figures
> Wandering here and there, devoid of reason,
> Anxious, in fear of death, and to advise them,
> And to make fate an open book.
>
> (tr. Rolfe Humphries)

The dangers correspond to the exultation. To teach seriously is to lay hands on what is most vital in a human being. It is to seek access to the quick and the innermost of a child's or an adult's integrity. A Master invades, he breaks open, he can lay waste in order to cleanse and to rebuild. Poor teaching, pedagogic routine, a style of instruction which is, consciously or not, cynical in its merely utilitarian aims, are ruinous. They tear up hope by its roots. Bad teaching is, almost literally, murderous and, metaphorically, a sin. It diminishes the student, it reduces to gray inanity the subject being presented. It drips into the child's or the adult's sensibility that most corrosive of acids, boredom, the marsh gas of ennui. Millions have had mathematics, poetry, logical thinking, killed for them by dead teaching, by the perhaps subconsciously vengeful mediocrity of frustrated pedagogues. Molière's vignettes are implacable.

Anti-teaching is statistically close to being the norm. Good teachers, fire-raisers in their pupils's nascent souls may well be rarer than virtuoso artists or sages. Schoolmasters, trainers of mind and body, aware of what is at stake, of the interplay of trust and vulnerability, of the organic fusion between responsibility and response (what I will call "answerability") are alarmingly few. Ovid reminds us: "there is no greater wonder." In actual fact, as we know, the majority of those to whom we entrust our children in secondary education, to whom we look for guidance and example in the academy, are more or less amiable gravediggers. They labour to diminish their students to their own level of indifferent fatigue. They do not "open Delphi" but close it.

The contrasting ideal of a true Master is no romantic fantasy or utopia out of practical reach. The fortunate among us will have met with true Masters, be they Socrates or Emerson, Nadia Boulanger or Max Perutz. Often, they remain anonymous: isolated school masters and mistresses who wake a child's or an adolescent's gift, who set obsession on its way. By lending a book, by staying after class willing to be sought out. In Judaism, the liturgy includes a special blessing for families at least one of whose offspring becomes a scholar.

How can vocation be put on a payroll? How is it possible to price revelation (*Dictaque mirantum magni primordia mundi*)? The question has haunted me and left me uneasy during my whole life as a teacher. Why have I been remunerated, given money, for what is my oxygen and *raison d'être?* To read with others, to study *Phaedrus* or *The Tempest,* to introduce (falteringly) *The Brothers Karamazov* around a table, to try to elucidate Proust's page on the death of Bergotte or a lyric by Paul Celan—these have been to me privileges, rewards, touches of grace and of hope like no others. What I now experience of retirement from teaching has left me orphaned. My doctoral seminar in Geneva ran, more or less unbroken, for a quarter of a century. Those Thursday mornings were as near as an ordinary, secular spirit can come to Pentecost. By what oversight or vulgarization should I have been paid to become what I am? When, and I have felt this with sharpening malaise, it might have been altogether more appropriate for me to pay those who invited me to teach?

Irate, derisive common sense cries out: teachers must *live,* even those high Masters, whom you probably romanticize, must *eat!* So many of them already suffer a wretched lot. To which unanswerable challenge an imp of the perverse, in an idiom not altogether of this world, murmurs: "living and eating are indeed absolute necessities, but also bleak and secondary in the light of the exploration and communication of the great and final things." Are there no alternatives to the professionalization, to the mercantilization of the Master's calling, to that equivalence between truth-seeking and salary introduced by the Sophists?

A society directed towards essentials could provide for the material necessities of its teachers. It was an arrangement of this kind which Socrates, with sovereign irony, proposed to his accusers. It would pay on a trade basis only and precisely the mediocre, those who have made a business of a calling. The Masters would be defrayed minimally, their enlistment being analogous to that of a mendicant friar. We shall see that hasidic Masters come within that sphere. More realistically, the Master, the thinker or questioner at large, will earn his daily bread in some manner disconnected from his vocation. Boehme made shoes, Spinoza polished lenses, Peirce—the most important philosopher so far produced by the New World—from the 1880s on produced his leviathan, formidably original works in direst poverty and isolation, Kafka and Wallace Stevens sat in their insurance offices, Sartre was a playwright, novelist, and pamphleteer of genius. Tenure is a trap and tranquillizer. A stringent academic system would require sabbaticals to be spent earning one's livelihood in a pursuit unrelated to one's speciality. Even if they apply only to a minority and postulate a community whose values are almost the antithesis to those now prevalent—the arrogance, the stench of money are pervasive—such scenarios are not impossible.

The questions raised coincide with the entry of the Sophists into the city. They arise out of the transition, far more gradual than we sometimes suppose, from orality to the book. This passage is enacted in the person and practices of Socrates. As are the dilemmas posed by the transition from the blessed anarchy of individual, "extramural" teaching to the rites of academe. Here, as well, the Sophists remain crucial. Our seminars come after Protagoras, our lectures after Gorgias.

◇◇◇

Commentaries, interpretations, scholarship are so compendious that not even the best qualified of Socratic and Platonic readers can achieve a complete view. Of the making of books, monographs, learned papers on Plato there is no end. Yet in all this industry one looks in vain for any comprehensive study of Socrates's relations to those whom he inspires, entrances, intrigues, exasperates. Attitudes towards Socrates encompass every nuance from adoration to murderous loathing. It is the psychological acumen, the subtlety in motion of these shadings and "sightlines" which defy classification. It is, I believe, more plausible to arrive at some ordered perception of the personae in Shakespeare than it is to circumscribe the prodigality, the intimacies and estrangements, of surrender and of rebellion in Plato's dialogues. At numerous points, Plato is a dramatist to rival Shakespeare; but the moral and intellectual energies are his (and perhaps Dante's) alone. Indeed, even in *Phaedo* and *Apology*, the straightforward question "are Socrates's interlocutors and listeners *disciples* in any obvious use of the word?" remains perplexing (sources in antiquity suggest that discipleship figures only late in Socrates's teaching).

Implicit is the insoluble challenge of the status or "truth-values" of Plato's portrayal. Time and again, the dialogues are offered as retrospective (impossibly) memorized narratives, at second or even at third hand. "A" communicates to "C" what he has heard from "B," in some cases pleading imperfect recollection or unverifiable transmission. Above all else, we shall never know to what extent the Platonic "Socrates" is just that: a *figura,* a poetic-philosophic construct whose density of presence, whose pressure of felt life is comparable if not superior to that which we experience in respect of Falstaff, of Hamlet, of Anna Karenina.

Plato had begun as a poet-dramatist. The dialogues are crowded with scenic circumstance—the banquet, the prison, the walk by the Ilissus river, the agora or street corner. They are paced around entrances and exits as significant as any in dramatic literature (Alcibiades bursting into Agathon's party). In ways as intricately plotted as Henry James's, Plato, in *Parmenides,* in *Protagoras,* in *Theaetetus,* alters the angles of incidence. Plato seems to invite the question: in what sense is he the author of the dialogue? Persistently, there are possibilities of distrust which we call deconstructive or postmodernist, of strategies of suspicion (*méfiance*) which may themselves symbolize aspects of Socratic irony and subversion. Yet at other moments, notably in *Crito, Phaedo,* and *Apology,* an immense directness, an immediacy of tragic feeling overwhelm us. These constitute one of the two principal passion plays ("mysteries") in western history. To borrow Wallace Stevens's phrase, Plato's Socrates—so different from Xenophon's or Aristophanes's—could be a "supreme fiction."

Did the historical Socrates, the individual done to death in 399 B.C., at a time of bitter internecine conflict in a defeated Athens, actually say the philosophically decisive, poignant words Plato ascribes to him? Aristophanes's *Clouds* testifies to what was comical, dubious in Socrates's reputation as a sophistic teacher and intellectual. Or was the Master, in fact, the robust moralist, the somewhat tedious pedagogue and landlocked spirit portrayed by Xenophon? The so-called "Socratic" dialogues by Antisthenes, Aristippus, Aeschines, Phaidon, and Eucleides are lost to us. Aristotle's witness is post facto (Plato met Socrates only in 408). Leo Strauss ponders whether "practically all details in the Platonic dialogues are invented yet the whole is literally true." The paradox is elegant but does not get us very far. The multiplicity, furthermore, and variousness of subsequent Socratic schools—the Cynics, the Hedonists, the school of Megara, the Platonic Academy—reveals how problematic, even self-contradictory, Socrates's teachings were felt to be. Finally, there is the extent, always debated, to which the dialogues reflect what may have been profound changes in Plato's metaphysical opinions (*doxa*), in his politics, in his dramatic rhetoric. In the last, arguably most engaged, of the dialogues, in *Laws,* Socrates is absent. This absence might mirror, in some almost unavowed counterpart, Plato's absence at the hour of Socrates's death.

No account of a disciple's feelings towards his Master excels that of Alcibiades. In the *Symposium,* Plato's stylistic virtuosity and scenic control are matchless. But hearing with any confidence what Alcibiades purports to tell us bristles with difficulties and traps. Not only is Alcibiades shown to us as "flown with wine" (the Miltonic "rioting in the streets" is exactly to the point), but his state is such as to enable him to use his drunkenness tactically. Moreover, Plato suggests that Alcibiades's sensibility on the night of Agathon's banquet is in that overwrought turbulent key which will, soon after, lead to personal and civic disaster.

Almost compulsively, Alcibiades insists on the Master's *strangeness:* "Such is Socrates's strangeness that you will search among those living now and among men of the past, and never come close to what he is himself and to the things he says." Alcibiades's (Plato's) depiction tells of a man of formidable bodily stamina, of indifference to danger when in combat. Socrates can consume quantities of wine while staying totally sober. This counterintuitive portrait denies the conventional identification of intellectual eminence and meditative abstraction with a fragile physique. It does foreshadow the excellence in war of an Alain or a Wittgenstein. In turn, Socrates's asceticism, his immunity to material needs and desires—Diogenes, observes Plato, was simply "Socrates gone mad"—will be reflected in Spinoza.

There is abiding strangeness in Socrates's recourse to his *daimonion,* to the tutelary spirit and familiar who attends on him at crucial junctures. It is this private oracle which sustains his commitment to the life of the mind, which inhibits him from entering politics. Elsewhere, this exemplar of sceptical rationality invokes Apollo and the Muses. A mocker of rhapsodes turns to poetry, to music as his end draws near. Socrates would have understood perfectly Wittgenstein's remark regarding the *Philosophical Investigations:* "If I could, I would dedicate this book to God." But how are we to gauge the part of irony, of self-teasing in Socrates's "daemonism" and/or more precisely in Plato's narrative? Were the Master's accusers justified when they sensed in the sage an ambiguous, conceivably negative or anarchic stance towards traditional, established faith? Certain Church Fathers were to discern in Socrates a creature of the devil; others hailed him as sanctified. The strangeness persists.

Alcibiades is vehement about Socrates's ugliness. The man is a bulbous, snub-nosed satyr, a Silenus. His countenance and body defy Attic criteria of masculine comeliness, of that physical lustre which tradition assigns to Plato. Yet the Master's powers of seduction are unrivalled; no one can withstand Socrates's charismatic spell, the witchcraft of his presence. It is from the image of Socrates, made immemorial by countless hellenistic and Roman busts, that Kierkegaard will derive the typology of the seducer. That seduction goes far beyond Socrates's words and dialectical entrapments. It is an undefinable composite, spiritual and carnal. The disciple is consumed with desire for his Master. Alcibiades's recital of his attempts to have sex with Socrates is of a wild, self-mocking humour and pain which defy paraphrase. Already, with a hint of fearful premonition, Socrates is on trial "on the charge of arrogance." The handsome Alcibiades has "lain all night with this godlike and extraordinary man" whom he desires and loves to the pitch of distraction. He has to leave him in the morning, frustrated by Socrates's ironic self-mastery "as if he had been my father or an elder brother."

Socrates is, to use an awkward term, an "eroticist." The nature, the quality of love, from lechery to transcendence (*agapē*) crowds his inquiries. The containment and unfolding of eros within the political, within the individual soul, the concord and conflicts between love and the philosophic pursuit of ultimate truths—these two must, at the last, be unified—is a leitmotif in the Platonic Socrates. Via Neoplatonism and hellenized Christianity, Socratic-Platonic eros will permeate western thought and sensibility. In actuality, Socratic love is homoerotic. It is the passion of an older man for an adolescent (among other texts, *Charmides* permits

no doubt as to the physical realities). Socrates's marriage to
Xanthippe becomes proverbial of wretchedness. Teachers of
philosophy may, now and again, have to do away with their
wives: witness the Althusser drama. It is with boys and their
radiant nakedness that Socrates finds fulfilment. Plato's own
views on homosexuality are difficult to make out, and the
whole subject remains contentious in classical studies and social anthropology. Its role, its significance in our entire theme
are eminent.

Eroticism, covert or declared, fantasized or enacted, is inwoven in teaching, in the phenomenology of mastery and
discipleship. This elemental fact has been trivialized by a
fixation on sexual harassment. But it remains central. How
could it be otherwise?

The pulse of teaching is persuasion. The teacher solicits attention, agreement, and, optimally, collaborative dissent. He
or she invites trust: "to exchange love for love and trust for
trust" as Marx put it, idealistically, in his 1844 manuscripts.
Persuasion is both positive—"share this skill with me, follow
me into this art and practise, read this text"—and negative—
"do not believe this, do not expend effort and time on that."
The dynamics are the same: to build a community out of
communication, a coherence of shared feelings, passions, refusals. In persuasion, in solicitation, be it of the most abstract, theoretical kind—the demonstration of a mathematical theorem, instruction in musical counterpoint—a process
of seduction, willed or accidental, is inescapable. The Master,
the pedagogue addresses the intellect, the imagination, the
nervous system, the very inward of his listener. When teaching physical skills, sport, musical performance, he addresses
the body. Address and reception, the psychological and the

physical are strictly inseparable (watch a ballet class at work). Totalities of mind and body are enlisted. A charismatic Master, an inspired "prof" take in hand, in a radically "totalitarian," psychosomatic grasp, the living spirit of their students or disciples. The dangers and privileges are unbounded.

Every "break-in" into the other, via persuasion or menace (fear is a great teacher) borders on, releases the erotic. Trust, offer and acceptance, have roots which are also sexual. Teaching and learning are informed by an otherwise inexpressible sexuality of the human soul. This sexuality eroticizes understanding and *imitatio.* Add to this the key point that in the arts and humanities the material being taught, the music being analysed and practised, are *per se* charged with emotions. These emotions will, in considerable part, have affinities, immediate or indirect, with the domain of love. I intuit that the solicitations in the sciences expend their own eros, though in ways more difficult to paraphrase.

A "master class," a tutorial, a seminar, but even a lecture can generate an atmosphere saturated with tensions of the heart. The intimacies, the jealousies, the disenchantments will shade into motions of love or of hatred or into complicated mixtures of both. The staging is one of desire and betrayal, of manipulation and detachment, as it is in the repertoire of eros. "You are the only lover I've ever had who's been really worthy of me," boasts Alcibiades, if only because Socrates, like any authentic Master, "is the only man in the world who can make me feel ashamed."

Over the millennia, in countless societies, the teaching situation, the transmission of knowledge, of techniques and of values (*paideia*) have knit in intimacy mature men and women on the one hand, adolescents and younger adults on

the other. It is in this ravelling that physical ugliness can seduce beauty; consider Michelangelo and Cavalieri. In the
Platonic Academy or Athenian gymnasium, in the Papuan
long house, in British public schools, in religious seminaries
of every hue, homoeroticism has not only flourished but been
regarded as educative. The erotic sway available to the *magister,* the sexual temptations exhibited, consciously or not, by
the pupil, polarize the pedagogic relation. I believe that there
inheres in effective teaching as in realised discipleship, an exercise of love or of that hatred which is the dark of love. In
ancient Athens, this exercise was openly pursued and philosophically underwritten. Also in Socrates, supreme embodiment of the erotic and of abstention. Again, this duality is
part of his "strangeness."

Strangest of all are Socrates's pedagogic methods, as reported by Plato. These have been the object of wonder or
derision, of philosophic and political speculation since
Aristophanes. The elenctic technique of question-and-answer
does not convey knowledge in any ordinary, didactic sense. It
aims to initiate in the respondent a process of uncertainty, a
questioning which deepens into a self-questioning. Socrates's
teaching is a refusal to teach, which may have been a distant
model for Wittgenstein. One might say that whoever grasps
Socrates's intention is made an autodidact, especially in ethics. For Socrates himself professes ignorance; the wisdom at-
tributed to him by the oracle at Delphi consists only in his
clear perception of his own unknowing.

Yet at what level of seriousness, of what Husserl would call
intentionality, is this celebrated avowal to be taken? Scholars
have argued the paradox interminably. At one or two points,
moreover, in *Meno* 98b, in *Apology* 29, Socrates claims cer-
tainty. Is there a fundamental sophistry in a profession of ig-

norance generating the teaching, the imparting of practical wisdom (Kant's *praktische Vernunft*)? A negation of knowledge can be interpreted as sagacity. The Socratic position, however, is not one of absolute relativism, let alone scepticism. The distinction between good and evil is urged untiringly. Socrates, unlike certain Sophist acrobats, refuses to put forward what he perfectly well knows—*eu oida*—to be evil. The whole ideal of the soul's equilibrium, *eudaimonia,* is founded on a compelling intuition of moral rectitude, of justice towards others and oneself. But can this be taught in any systematic, institutional manner? "Teach at Harvard? It cannot be done," opined Ezra Pound.

Plato's advocacy of experts in virtue is not, I conjecture, Socratic. For Socrates, true teaching is by example. It is, literally, exemplary. The meaning of the just life lies in living it. In ways very difficult to define, a dialectical exchange with Socrates, an experiencing of him (an opaque phrasing) enacts the examined, hence just life. Wittgenstein's *Tractatus* may help when it insists on meaning as "showing," as "ostensible." A Socratic moral elicitation is an act of "pointing towards."

A good many of the ambushes that Socrates sets for his listeners are, in fact, shallow and refutable. One bridles at the Platonic transcriptions of monosyllabic assent. That, however, is not the point. We learn by watching an athlete perform or a musician play. In some ideal fiction, a mute Socrates is conceivable; or one who dances his meaning, as would Zarathustra. Here also, the finale of the *Tractatus* is pertinent.

In *Euthydemus* and, most expressly, in *Meno,* the Platonic Socrates comes close to cancelling out the function, the reality of teaching as we customarily define them. "A man cannot inquire about what he knows, because he knows it, and in that case he is in no need of inquiry; nor, again, can he inquire about what he does not know, since he does not know what he is to inquire." It follows that knowledge is recollection. Being immortal, the soul has learned all things (*chrēmata*) in a prior state of existence. All things being related, it can recapture the components of knowledge via contiguity and association (how near Socrates is, at moments, to Freud). Discovery equals recovery, the "recovery by oneself of knowledge latent within oneself." Are there in this model ironized vestiges of Orphic and Pythagorean doctrines?

The Socratic teacher is, famously, a midwife to the pregnant spirit, an alarm clock rousing us from amnesia, from what Heidegger would call "a forgetting of Being." The Master induces visions which are, in effect, re-visions and déjà-vu. But how, in that case, is error possible? And it has been shown that the geometrical proof that Socrates elicits by his midwifery from the slave boy in *Meno* is unsound. What prevails is the motif of a creative sleeplessness. The Zen Master beats his disciples to keep them awake. Great teaching is insomnia, or ought to have been in the Garden at Gethsemane. Sleepwalkers are the natural enemies of the teacher. In *Meno,* Anytus, alert to the subversive, unsettling tactics of Socratic pedagogy, admonishes: "Be circumspect." But no committed Master can be. Where there is acute discomfort—Socratic questioning can numb like "a stingray" says *Meno* 84—there is also love. Hölderlin conveys it perfectly in his "Sokrates und Alcibiades":

> "Warum huldigest du, heiliger Sokrates,
> > Diesem Jünglinge stets? kennst du Größers nicht?
> > > Warum sieht mit Liebe,
> > > > Wie auf Götter, dein Aug auf ihn?"

Wer das Tiefste gedacht, liebt das Lebendigste,
  Hohe Jugend versteht, wer in die Welt geblickt,
    Und es neigen die Weisen
      Oft am Ende zu Schönem sich.

"Why holy Socrates, do you pay tribute
  Constantly to this youth? Do you know nothing greater?
    Why, with love,
      Does your eye look on him as on gods?"

Who has thought deepest, loves that which is most alive,
  Who has looked into the world, understands elect youth,
    And oft', at the end, the wise
      Incline towards the beautiful.

◇◇◇

A writer of genius, Plato, in *Phaedrus* and the *Seventh Letter,* advocates orality. Only the spoken word and face-to-face can elicit truth and, *a fortiori,* guarantee honest teaching. It is an unsettling paradox, but in the author of the dialogues, the suspicion in regard to the invention of writing and to any written *doxa* runs deep.

Writing induces a neglect, an atrophy of the arts of memory. But it is memory which is "the Mother of the Muses," the human endowment that makes possible all learning. This proposition is at once psychological and, as we have seen in the thesis on the preexistence and immortality of the soul in *Meno,* metaphysical. In the Platonic construct of Ideas and ideal Forms, understanding and futurity are a "commemoration," an act of remembrance whose generative energies are oral. In a more general vein: that which we know *by heart* will ripen and deploy within us. The memorized text interacts with our temporal existence, modifying our experiences, being dialectically modified by them. The stronger the muscles of memory, the better guarded our integral self. Neither censor nor state police can uproot the remembered poem (witness the survival, from mouth to mouth, of Mandelstam's poems where no written version was feasible). In the death camps, certain rabbis and Talmudic scholars were known to be "living books," the pages of whose total recall could be "turned" by other inmates in search of judgement or consolation. Major epic literature, the founding myths begin to decay with the "advance" into writing. On all these counts, the detergence of memory in today's schooling is grimy stupidity. Consciousness is casting overboard its vital ballast.

Secondly, writing arrests, immobilizes discourse. It renders static the free play of thought. It enshrines a normative but factitious authority. The Mosaic law stems from a second set of Tables untouched by the living hand of God. Antigone argues the unwritten justice (*themis*) "inscribed" but unwritten in the human soul against the prescriptive legality (*nomoi*) of Creon's despotism. The written word does not listen to its reader. It takes no account of his questions and objections. A speaker can correct himself at every point; he can amend his message. The book sets its *main morte* on our attention. *Auctoritas* stems from authorship.

Fascinatingly, the interactive, correctible, interruptable media of word processors, of electronic textualities on the internet and the web, may amount to a return, to what Vico would call a *ricorso,* to orality. Screened texts are, in some sense, provisional and open-ended. These conditions may restore factors of authentic teaching as practised by Socrates and dramatized by Plato. At the same time, however, electronic literacy, with its limitless capacity for information storage and retrieval, with its data banks, militates against memory. And the face on the screen is never that live countenance which Plato or Levinas judge indispensable in any fruitful encounter between Master and disciple.

Orality may infer a distinction between teaching and revelation, though these categories overlap. Even when it is verbally disclosed, revelation often cites a sacred, canonic source which is itself textual. It relates to a Torah, a Gospel, a Koran, or Book of Mormon. Dictation in letters of fire underwrites the Sinaitic revelation, the Book of Revelation taken down by St. John on Patmos, the holy red writ of Maoism. Only the presupposition of a graphic act and witness can empower the revealed message. There is, in this sense, no more "revealed" epiphany, so Talmudic in its lineaments, than that of the Marxist creed. Oral teaching, on the other hand, burgeons with creative errors, with the resources of amendment and rebuttal. Revealed verities, with their bookish source—a "Bible," Mallarmé's *le Livre* which contains the universe—turn thought to marble. Having been dictated, instruction is not so much "didactic" as it is "dictatorial" (together with "edict," these words form an ominous constellation).

"A fine teacher, but didn't publish": this is the punch line to a macabre Harvard joke on Jesus of Nazareth's inaptness for tenure. In the background looms a momentous fact. Neither Socrates nor Jesus commit their teachings to the written word. Only twice throughout Plato does the Master resort to consulting a scroll; in neither case, is he the author. The single, enigmatic exception occurs in John 8:1–8. Questioned by the Pharisees concerning a woman taken in adultery, "Jesus stooped down, and with his fingers wrote on the ground, as though he heard them not." He does so a second time after his radiant challenge: "let him who is without sin cast the first stone." We learn nothing of what he wrote in the dust or as to what tongue it was in. Almost from the outset, this mysterious pericope has been suspect. Scholars now regard it as a later interpolation to be excised. We have no evidence that Jesus could write.

It is no hyperbole to say that Socrates and Jesus stand at the pivot of our civilization. The passion narratives inspired by their deaths generate the inward alphabets, the encoded recognitions of much of our moral, philosophic, and theological idiom. They remain transcendental even in largely immanent spaces and have instilled in western awareness both an irremediable sadness and a fever of hope. Similitudes, parallels, contrasts between the two begetters have marshalled religious exegeses, moral and philosophic hermeneutics, but also the study of poetic genres and dramatic techniques. It is virtually impossible to grasp the motions of the western intellect from Herder to Hegel, from Kierkegaard to Nietzsche and Lev Shestov, without the informing presence of Socrates and of Jesus. The dual iconography is equally extensive. Socrates's raised finger in the hour of his farewell in Jacques-Louis David's celebrated painting is deliberately antecedent to that of Jesus.

My focus here is on teaching, on Mastery and discipleship, in Athens and in Galilee and Jerusalem. The itinerant pedagogue, the virtuoso dialectician out of Nazareth, tells all who would listen that he is nothing more and nothing less than a teacher.

Unlike Socrates, the Galilean Master chooses and enlists his disciples. Their number pertains to inherited numerology: initially, they are twelve, as are the tribes of Israel and the signs of the zodiac. They are not the aristocrats or golden youths of Athens, but common folk: "And they were astonished at his doctrine: for he taught them as one that had authority, and not as the scribes."

Where much of Platonic *doxa,* voiced by Socrates, is articulated via myths, the marrow of Jesus's teaching inheres in parables—an oral shorthand addressed to memorization. The epistemological status of these two modes, their validity and "truth functions," have been argued over perennially. A cardinal definition of genius points, I believe, to the capacity to originate myths, to devise parables. This capacity is exceedingly rare. It marks Kafka rather than Shakespeare, Wagner rather than Mozart. Platonic-Socratic myths, such as that of the Cave, the mustard-seed or prodigal son parables of Jesus, share certain features. They are open-ended in that they provoke inexhaustible multiplicities and potentialities of interpretation. They keep the human spirit off-balance. They elide our paraphrase and understanding even as we seem to grasp them (this is, precisely, Heidegger's model of *aletheia,* of a truth which conceals itself in the very process of disclosure). The myth of the charioteer, the parable of the sower are perfectly bounded yet limitless. Relativity physics can handle this apparent contradiction. It may be that the myths in Plato and the parables in the Gospels are, at their secret core, unfolding metaphors. This dynamic is operative in Kafka's transparent yet fathomless parable of the Law. An analogy might be that of perfectly meaningful, applicable undecidability in mathematics.

But "analogy," itself so slippery a notion, does not get us very far. Like almost no others, the myths recounted by Plato, the parables offered by Jesus, incarnate—I use the word designedly—what is at once decisive and inexplicable in Mastery, in the art of teaching. The hunger of the soul, of the intellect, for meaning, compels the disciple (ourselves) to come back, over and again, to these texts. This return, always frustrated yet always reborn, may take us as near as is possible to the concept of resurrection. Which is also, I venture, a metaphor.

The nuances, the economy of reference and personal context, make it almost impossible to arrive at any systematic ordering of Socrates's students and acolytes. A two-dimensional technique in the synoptic Gospels provides a number of Jesus's disciples with incisive immediacy. Like figures in Byzantine mosaics, they are at once flat and monumental. Millennia of liturgical invocation and exegeses, moreover, have afforded a Peter, an Andrew, a Simon the Canaanite their individuation. Where would painting, architecture in the west be without them? There are in Jesus spurts of impatience, even of violence. They can be directed at the disciples. James and John are reproved. Peter's betrayal is foretold. A would-be follower is commanded to abandon his father's burial—an exigence which drastically severs Jesus of Nazareth from what is virtually the holiest obligation in Judaism. The Master's anger rings out: "Peter, Simon, sleepest thou, could you not watch an hour?" Once again, that theme of sleeplessness as it attaches to great teaching.

I have tried to show elsewhere (cf. *No Passion Spent,* 1996) how close are the structural parallels between the *Symposium* and the Last Supper narratives. In both there is a dramaturgy of exits and entrances; both evoke the pressures of political-social turbulence in the surrounding night. Martyrdom, imminent in the one case, on the horizon in the other, shadows every move in the house of Agathon and in "the large upper room furnished" for Passover in Jerusalem. Nothing is trivialized if one of the approaches we take to these two nocturnes is that of a seminar or master class.

Indeed, this perspective may throw psychological light on the blackest of themes. The non-Christian has little access to Jesus's motiveless choice of Judas for damnation, to the identification of Judas with money (he is bursar to the disciples). For Jews, till this day, the consequences will be hideous. There is, however, a possible impulse in Judas himself which we will come up against throughout the history of Mastery and discipleship. This relationship is charged with rivalry among disciples. Each aches to be the Master's favourite, to become his elect dauphin. There is no coven, no atelier, no university seminar, no research team in which that aspiration and the jealousies it engenders are absent. Alcibiades bears vehement witness to this impulse. It is no different, more than two thousand years later, in the tragic imbroglio of Gershom Scholem and Jakob Taubes. Suicide can ensue. The Last Supper tells of the disciple "whom Jesus loved" (*hon egapa*). Depicted in western art as "leaning on Jesus's bosom," this personage remains unidentified. *Eine Idealgestalt,* says Bultmann; a *figura esoterico-misterica,* a "beloved" to whom Jesus confides words inaudible to the other disciples.

The Gospels hint at Judas's flawed love for his Master, at his desire to be singled out, a desire so atrociously fulfilled.

He accepts the morsel which signals his anathema. It is, so certain commentaries, a "Satanic sacrament" in irreparable antithesis to that of communion. Judas has been compelled to witness Jesus's election to manifest love of one whom tradition will designate as "John" and whom certain mystical hierarchies will set above Peter. A raw humanity breaks through in Judas's disappointment and jealousy. Iago and Othello. Half inebriate, half self-condemned, Alcibiades will leave the Master and outrage the city. Judas Iscariot goes "immediately" into that night (*en de nux*) from which his people have never truly emerged. Where the particular choice and love by the Master are supremely striven for, rejection is unbearable. All that is left to the disciple with the red hair and the hooked nose is the purse which—the ironies are grim—the Master has entrusted to him.

We do not know why Plato was absent at Socrates's death, *pace* David's painting, or, more precisely, why he excludes himself from *Crito,* in which that death is recounted. Could the pain have been too great (Socrates bids the disciples contain their lament)? Paul of Tarsus never laid eyes on Jesus. By force of written language, the two disciples assured their Masters' posthumous immensity. Orality was published and made durable. But at a price which is reflected in the emblematic opposition between the spirit and the letter. Plato's mature teachings and metaphysics deviate more and more from what we know of Socrates. Paul transmutes Jesus of Nazareth into Christ. This transformative process is a recurrent, even central element in the lessons of the Masters. Fidelity and betrayal are close knit.

2

RAIN OF FIRE

◇ ◇ ◇

HENCEFORTH, two sovereign currents intertwine: Christianity and Neoplatonism. Christendom will claim for its own Plato's *anima naturaliter christiana.* Its own symbolism and transcendental abstractions are often Neoplatonism made scenic. The synapse is Plotinus.

The Master will teach for twenty-six years in Rome, renewing Platonism in a period of social-political menace. Like his own teacher, Ammonius, Plotinus does not write. But the disciples in what Augustine will call a *Plotini schola* take down his oral instruction. They bear witness to a radically charismatic experience, to what Dante, indirectly influenced by Plotinus, identifies in *Paradiso* as a "luce intelletual piena d'amore." The reputed nine hundred books of scholia recorded by Amelius are lost to us, but Plotinus's doctrines and pedagogy have endured. The Master "seemed ashamed of being in a body" (this, we will see, is axiomatic to Alain, *maître à penser*). Modelling his ideals on those of Pythagoras, he

advocates asceticism, a vegetarian diet, abstinence from too
much sleep, and celibacy. Again in the style of Pythagoras
and, some have argued, of Plato himself, Plotinus's teachings
are two-tiered: esoteric *doxa* is confided to an elite of initiates;
exoteric discourse is addressed to listeners at large. Auditors
assembled from far and wide. They included three Senators,
physicians, a learned poet, a rhetorician notorious for usury
and avarice. Women were made welcome on an equal footing
(it is Pauline Christianity with its rabbinic antecedents that
institutes the great barrier). A handful of philosophers are in
attendance. We know of disciples who renounce the world in
the Master's image.

The message is one of harmonic unison. *Contra* existential
Gnosticism and its Manichaeian cosmology, Plotinus urges
the soul towards homecoming, towards a return to infinite
oneness. "Perhaps Evil is merely an impediment to the Soul
like something affecting the eye and so hindering sight." A
dictum which will inspire Spinoza who instructs us that serious philosophic inquiry is the sole authentic life; the rest "is a
toy." Yet this ideal of harmony, and the manifest luminosity
of the Master's presence were, it would appear, accompanied
by extreme psychic tension. At least one scholar speaks of
the nervousness, of the pathological disturbances occasioned
among Plotinus's disciples by the untiring stress of metaphysical meditation. (The phenomenon will recur in Wittgenstein's coven.)

We owe our knowledge of Plotinus's lectures and seminars
to a document almost unique in classical writings: the biographical and autobiographical *vita* with which Porphyry
prefaces his redaction of the *Enneads*. Elements of formulaic
hagiography are obvious, as are imitations of both Pythag-

orean and Socratic-Platonic antecedents. Nevertheless, Porphyry's account is invaluable. Seminars proceeded in the manner of a *conversazione,* of a free exchange innocent of "professorial pomp." Some of the Master's pronouncements were so lofty, ethically or theoretically demanding, that listeners did not dare ask for elucidation. At moments Plotinus seemed in dialogue "with his indwelling spirit, a Being of divine degree" (cf. Socrates's *daimonion*). Normally, however, he invited objections and was lucid and powerful in meeting them. He organised banquets in honour of Socrates and Plato—a practise to be mimed, in turn, by Stefan George. Speeches were delivered in recollection of the *Symposium,* but Plotinus condemned utterly Alcibiades's profession of carnal submission. No one, as Longinus testified, had thrown a clearer light on the principles of Pythagoras and of Plato, translating these into precepts of personal conduct, of trust in the immortality, albeit mysterious, of the human essence. It was via his manner of mastery that Plotinus enacted his doctrine of divine "emanations." The Plotinian heritage was to be prodigal. A Latin selection from the treatises set St. Augustine on his way. Boethius prepares the authority of Plotinus in Giordano Bruno, in the Florentine Neoplatonism of Marsilio Ficino. Plotinus's "monism" inspires Berkeley, Schelling, and Hegel. Bergson, in his vitalist teachings, is a distant disciple. Stephen Mackenna's rhapsodic translation and Plotinus's praeternaturalism surface in Yeats.

The close was tragic. Afflicted by ill health (leprosy?), Plotinus withdrew into the Campania, where he had once hoped to found a city based on Plato's *Laws.* Death found him in virtual isolation. In 268 A.D., the murder of Emperor Gallianus, his patron and friend, triggered a reign of terror.

The disciples scattered (Plato is absent at Socrates's final hour, St. Peter denies Jesus). In Rome, the realm of the spirit and of the intellect had been extinguished. Plotinus seems to have been haunted by the doom of Priam. Certain of the disciples sought to carry on in Syria. Had their Master not taught that "misfortune stimulates philosophic investigations"? The oracle at Delphi had declared Socrates's wisdom. Now, according to Porphyry, Apollo raised "an undying song" to the memory of "a gentle friend, Plotinus . . . Sleep never closed those eyes . . . you saw sights many and fair not granted to all that labour in wisdom's quest." Plotinus's "hallowed soul had risen above the bitter waves of this blood-drenched life."

Iamblichus had parted company. He found unacceptable the underlying rationalism of Plotinus's readings of Plato. His bent was that of a mystagogue. His *De vita Pythagorica liber,* however, illustrates a pedagogy close to that of the Master. Students lived with or near Iamblichus. They met with him daily and shared meals. Texts by Plato and Aristotle were assigned for close study and discussion. Even where the flavour was one of theurgy and of a Pythagorean mystique eight centuries after the fact, Iamblichus's methods were also philological. He was protesting the rights of immanent, if inspired, speculation as against the dogmatism of the Christian churches. Thus it is, in the catastrophic circumstances of the third and fourth centuries that philosophic-academic techniques still in force today have their origins.

Recurrently, Augustine brings his introspective powers to bear on the magisterial. Had the redoubtable Anselm of Milan not been his mentor? But a special gravity attaches to *De magistro.* The partner in this spacious dialogue is Augustine's son Adeotatus. The work was composed between 388 and 391.

The boy, whom the *Confessions* recall as exceptionally gifted, had died in 389, aged seventeen. Our text, with its emphasis on the transit from the bodily to the spiritual, *per corporalia ad incorporalia,* is also an *in memoriam.* Augustine's central thesis is Platonic. Soul and intellect must be "drilled" so as to awake them towards the apprehension of eternal, revealed truths. The indispensable, preliminary step towards such understanding is semiotic, the study of "signs." Without signs there is no access to meaning. Yet in themselves, signs "teach nothing." This paradox necessitates the Augustinian construct of "the inward Master." Which is to say the sole "Master of truth" who is Christ.

Citations from Scripture, notably from St. Paul, abound. But the argument on semantics draw principally on Cicero and the Roman grammarians. These, in turn, are encased in the larger issues of philosophical dialectics, of the elucidation of signification and meaning. The crux is the Christianized Platonism of the inner light. Positing this "special incorporeal light," Augustine amends and goes beyond *Meno.* The Platonism here may have been indirect, with Plotinus as intermediary. Already, however, Origen and Ambrose had dwelt on Matthew 23:10: "You have only one Master, Christ." Augustine purposes to apply this axiom to the communication of thought and of knowledge (*paideia*) as a whole. Hence an unprecedented, as it were technical, concern with the limitations and enigmas of semantic means. How is teaching possible?

In the ninth book of *Confessions,* Augustine looks back on his past as a teacher of rhetoric and forensic skills. This praxis had been nothing except "a marketplace of gossip." It had been sophistry. Any worthwhile *magisterium* entails a triangular relationship. The apex but also the base are those of immutable, divine verity. As Augustine summarizes in his *Sermons:* "We speak, but it is God who teaches" (Gerard Manley Hopkins looks back to this distinction). Christ's incarnation takes on a rigorously pedagogic function: "the sole interior Master has externalized himself so as to summon us from the external to the internal." What has been a transcendental, almost mythopoetic abstraction in Plato, becomes material. The wonder of signs, of their capacity to signify and transmit, relates immediately to the living Word, to the Logos that is the Johannine Christ. From grammar and grammatology, we have proceeded to philosophic theology. It is fair to say that for Augustine language is indeed "sign language." Wittgenstein will have recourse to Augustine when he puts forward his model of ostensible definition. But Augustine is acutely aware of the paradox of self-reference, of the sign pointing only to itself in an unbreakable hermeneutic circle: *quae tamen cum etiam ipsa signum sit.* Via words we learn nothing but words: *verbis igitur nisi verba non discimus.* Deconstructionists and postmodernists are faithless Augustinians.

As in current transformational generative theories of language, semantic capacities are, for Augustine, innate. But this innateness is not physiological. Faith must precede grammar and the means of understanding. The Word which is Christ quite literally "inhabits" the human psyche, though that indwelling needs to be liberated by grace. Individual resources will differ and determine the compass of intelligible insight. But via "a secret and simple perception," *secreto ac simplici oculo,* the listener will achieve understanding and assent. In this process the Master's instruction will serve as a catalyst;

but, as in *Meno,* the acts of apprehension must derive from the disciple's energized contemplation. Questioning wakes knowledge and emulation which were present *a priori.* Authentic students are *discipuli veritatis.* How then are error and misprision possible? How do liars and deceivers operate? The fault lies with the fallibility of the semantic, with the proclivity of discourse towards concealment and diversion. This ambiguity inherent in speech acts obsessed Augustine and elicited many of his most penetrating analyses.

Listening to his Master, the disciple ponders the lesson *pro viribus intuentes,* via the strengths of understanding afforded him by an inner light. Too often, disciples laud their Masters when, in a sense, they should be praising themselves (*non se doctores potius laudare, quam doctos*). The seeming immediacy of the learning process, the flash of the self-evident, conceal the miraculous origins and complexity of the phenomenon. Throughout, the validation is transcendent. For there is only one true Master: *quod unus omnium magister in caelis sit* ("the only true critic," says Hopkins of Christ). Education is simply our ability, our readiness to turn to Him. Where these are not enlisted, doctrine and pedagogy are sophistry. Thus the maieutic method of Socrates, as narrated by Plato, is an allegoric anticipation of Christian teaching. Already the "unknown God" encountered by St. Paul in Corinth was at work.

The entire model, given pressure by personal circumstance, arises out of an experience which is close to despair. Like Pascal after him, Augustine is haunted by the relativism, by the uncertainties of all rhetoric, where "rhetoric" and strategies of enticement are somehow inseparable from even the best-intentioned of teachings. Augustine experienced with peculiar edge the duplicities of the charismatic. His nose for seduction was acute. "Beware of the great teacher"; tenure is never to be unguardedly trusted.

◇◇◇

Shakespeare's inventory of experience is, justly, held to be unsurpassed. What trade, what craft or vocation—that of the physician, the lawyer, the moneylender, the soldier, the navigator, the soothsayer, the whore, the divine, the politician, the joiner, the musician, the criminal, the sanctified, the farmer, the peddlar, the monarch—escaped his notice? Silly books have been written about Shakespeare's inexplicable familiarity with statecraft, with diplomacy, with the arts of war. What order of human relations lay outside his intuitions? His is the sum of the world. Yet so far as we can tell, the theme we are concerned with, that of Masters and disciples, left Shakespeare indifferent.

Holofernes, in *Love's Labour's Lost,* is a stock figure out of Roman comedy; his pedantry is routinely satirized. There is (embarrassed) malice in the treatment of Polonius's sententious didacticism. If Shakespeare attends at all to Mastery and discipleship, it is in respect of Prospero. Caliban is harshly schooled. A severe love informs the education of Miranda. But these are not central motifs. Yet I suspect that if we could account for this omission we might gain access to vital areas in Shakespeare's labyrinthine sensibility. As is, "we ask and ask" (Matthew Arnold).

It is banal to observe in Shakespeare an unparalleled capacity for immediate grasp, for catching even specialized, technical material on the wing. A passing hint, a trick of language or of gesture registered perhaps casually, initiate constellations of association, of metaphoric congruence, at once penetrating and comprehensive. Cast wide, the language net draws in and fuses "infinite variety." Might the absence from the canon of the dramas of Mastery and discipleship, as these would have been familiar to Shakespeare from Scripture and Plutarch, point to the rebuke, be it subconscious, of the self-taught universalist to the claims, to the pretentions of mandarin authority? Though in a different vein, we find this reflex also in Montaigne. The contrast with that hunger after formal learning which animates Ben Jonson, George Chapman, and, we shall see, Christopher Marlowe, is pointed.

The *Sonnets,* moreover, enact a chronicle of self-education, a discipline for the unquiet heart in regard to itself so intense, so psychologically innovative and astute, as to render superfluous, indeed trivial the dialectic of scholastic instruction. Who could have *taught* Shakespeare the truths and falsehoods of human consciousness?

Should there be any merit to these conjectures, light might be thrown on the perennial issue of Shakespeare's agnosticism, on the elision of any credo which we could identify as his own (this vacuum exasperated readers such as Verdi and Wittgenstein). Transcendent privacy hedges Shakespeare's beliefs:

> And thou, who didst the stars and sunbeams know,
> Self-school'd, self-scann'd, self-honour'd, self-secure,
> Didst tread on earth unguess'd at.—Better so!

Arnold may be right. But the difference from Dante could not be greater.

There are multiple approaches to the *Commedia,* all incomplete. One reading is to construe the work as an epic of learning. By virtue of progressive encounters whose psychological finesse and drama are matched only by Plato, the intellect, agent of the Pilgrim's soul, ascends from darkest bewilderment to the limits of human understanding which are exactly those of language. Dante is "scholastic" in every sense of the term. He is supremely learned, in a thoroughly academic vein. Even at its most fervent, his sensibility conceptualizes. His genius for myth and lyric articulation is innervated by logic, by technical rhetoric and analytic scruple. He makes abstraction fiery. From *Vita Nuova* onward, Dante feels thought and thinks feeling.

The springs, the *moto spirituale* of the *Commedia* are those of pedagogy. The poem instructs as it unfolds, this deployment being couched in successive lessons and master classes. Mastery and discipleship are elemental to the journey. The ultimate *mio maestro* is an Inaccessible Deity. But as in the geometry of tangents—Dante's own analogy—or as in differential calculus, mortal apprehension closes in on the centre. Successive "singing masters of the soul" (Yeats) inform, nurture, correct, discipline, and praise the disciple. There is hardly a branch of transmission, of didactic method, of formal and exemplary schooling, that Dante leaves unexplored. To "educate" signifies "to lead forth," be it through the kindergartens of Hell. (Damnation is one mask of childishness.)

Surely, all this has been noted before. But the wonder of it bears repeating.

Dante was himself a star pupil: of the Sicilian school, of the Provençal troubadours, of such immediate predecessors and contemporaries as Guinizelli and Cavalcanti. He looked to Aquinas and the Aristotle of the scholastics for certification. Virgil's talismanic, Sybilline status was established. Had his Fourth Eclogue not prefigured, by intuition of grace, the birth of Christ? Had he not heralded (*"nostra maggior musa"*) the destined splendours of imperial, papal Rome? Dante's radical and determinant stroke was to make of the author of the *Aeneid* the Pilgrim's guide, father figure, exemplar. The elective partnership between Master and disciple becomes the axis of the journey. The density of interaction, of articulate and subconscious sharing is such that any adequate treatment would mean, virtually, a verse-by-verse rereading of both *Inferno* and *Purgatorio.* The pupillage is declared at the outset: "Tu sei lo mio maestro e 'l mio autore." Centuries later, a Platonic absolutist and passionate connoisseur of Dante, Pierre Boutang, will write to Charles Maurras, then in prison and national disgrace: "Mon cher maître, mon maître, jamais ce beau mot n'a été plus complètement vrai que dans le rapport que j'ai à vous"—"My dear master, my master, never has that lovely word been truer than in the relation I have with you." The *Commedia* is the anatomy of that rapport. More than any text thereafter, is it our *Bildungsroman.* It knows of the sadness inherent in all paternity, of the shadow of betrayal thrown where the light of welcome, of fidelity (*"onore e lume"*) is most concentrated.

As Mandelstam noted in his inspired gloss on the *Commedia,* Dante's resort to numerology cuts deep. His sensibility enumerates. Ninety citations of Virgil in *Inferno,* thirty-four in *Purgatorio,* only thirteen in *Paradiso.* This minutely gauged *diminuendo* calibrates the fading of the disciple's dependence on his Master, of the *Commedia*'s debts to the *Aeneid.* (These two recessions are complementary.) Direct translations from Virgil occur seven times in Hell, five times in Purgatory, but once only in the heavenly sphere. In counterpoint, Scripture is translated a dozen times in Paradise, where it is at home, eight times in Purgatory, but once only in the abyss. Moreover, allusions to the *Aeneid* in the eighth and ninth cantos of *Paradiso* are abrasive. Pagan mastery is no longer welcome.

The "tragedy in the 'Commedia,'" in Robert Holland's telling phrase, is incipent in *Inferno* I. Virgil's irreparable exile from salvation is made manifest. This fact will be eclipsed but never cancelled by the celebration of trust: "And when he had placed his hand on mine, with a cheerful look from which I took comfort, he led me among the secret things." Persistently, the terrified, ignorant Pilgrim, childlike, will turn to his Master—"io mi volsi al mar di tutto 'l senno"—"I turned to the sea of all wisdom." But the flaw in the crystal can already be heard towards the finale of canto IX, when an Angel intercedes to rescue both Master and disciple from satanic perils. The evocation of necromancy and monstrosity out of Lucan's *Pharsalia* subtly delimits Virgil's realm. Christ has "broken" history and time. However privileged, neither Virgil's descent into Hades via the *Aeneid* nor his guidance in Dante's epic, are those of Christ's harrowing. Yet in this very same twelfth canto, Theseus and Hercules are licensed to anticipate on Christ's triumphant militancy. Dante rarely lets us relax in the straightforward.

The first crisis occurs in XIII.46–51. The challenge is momentous: to what degree are the precedents enacted, narrated in the *Aeneid* trustworthy? The question is posed at a stage in medieval classicism when quotations from Virgil, randomly chosen, could carry oracular credibility. I am simplifying a dialectic of exceeding intricacy. What, inquires Dante, is *fiction* itself, is "that truth which has the face of a lie" (XVI.124)?

The *Commedia,* Dante insists, is "true invention." A distinction, at once vulnerable and of overwhelming import, is being urged as between "true fiction" and what might be entitled "mendacious verity." Fictive truths, as in the *Commedia,* are authorized, are to be credited, through a providential, retrospective awareness of the rebirth of imagination and of intellect in Christ's coming. Canto XX discriminates—has there been any more acute philological critic than Dante?—between orders of myth and feigning in the four Latin Masters we first met in Limbo. Statius, Ovid, Lucan, Virgil himself are inspired poets; but they are "seers unblest" and, therefore, ultimately false. No metamorphosis equals transubstantiation.

What ensues is among the most arresting conceits in literature. Faced by palpable proof of Christ's agency in Hell, Virgil corrects the prophecy uttered by Manto in the *Aeneid.* A supreme Master confesses error and corrects his own work. Is there any other example of this proceeding before the pallid games played in Gide's *Counterfeiters?* What in our modernism is as deconstructive? From that instant forward, the disciple's submission to his loved Master modulates into questioning.

Purgatorio develops a deepening critique of the concept of *fama,* of secular glory beyond death as it had been affirmed by the Master in *Inferno* XXIV. The high drama of valediction in fact extends across sixty-four cantos. Virgil, who has converted Statius to Christianity, whose Fourth Eclogue is annunciation, remains resistant to the Saviour's law ("ribellante a la sua legge"). In Book IX of *Inferno,* he doubts Beatrice's divine commission and safeguard. What the Pilgrim-disciple intuits is a mysterious *faillimento* which inhibits his Master from acting on his own clairvoyance. Very much as in Kierkegaard, the aesthetic has ordained limitations. Grace, theologically understood, generates the transition from even the perfection of formal beauty (the *Aeneid*) to the sacrament of love. In the dramaturgy of the *Commedia,* four pagans are allowed salvation: Statius and Cato in Purgatory, Traiano and Rifeo in Paradise. Medieval mythography would have given Dante ample license to "save" Virgil. Yet the disciple consigns his "dolicissime patre"—the sole use of that superlative in the entire epic—to "the ancient race in ancient error" ("le genti antiche ne l'antico errore"). Virgil had not heard the Word in the verb. Virgil himself mourns his "relegation to eternal exile." Dante's intransigence has puzzled, irritated many of his best readers. What opaque betrayal is at work? (What "Oedipal vengeance," would be the psychoanalytic phrasing.)

Whatever the motives, the enactment of farewell takes the *Commedia* to its highest pitch of *literary* pathos. No adieu surpasses the executive virtuosity and truth of feeling in *Purgatorio* XXX. Trembling at the approach of the new Master-Mistress, Beatrice, the Pilgrim turns to the *Aeneid.* Recognizing in himself "the signs of ancient ardour," he cites Virgil's original: "adgnosco veteris vestigia flammae." Dido recalls her former love for Sicheo. The only other *auctor* whom Dante quotes "in the original" is God. The enlistment of quotation comes close to defining a culture. The *Commedia* cannot be without the *Aeneid* (St. Paul cites Euripides), but must amend it. Proclaiming the efficacy of Christian prayer, Beatrice deliberately misquotes the famous dictum of despair in the sixth book of the *Aeneid.* Despair is counter-Christian. Virgil has known how to "make light"—"facere luce"—but Beatrice *is* light.

In the actual farewell of disciple to Master, there is a strong echo of Virgil's *Georgics*. Scholars now believe that Dante knew this work. Orpheus's farewell to Eurydice becomes that of the Pilgrim to his guide. The Pilgrim weeps knowing that his Master must, like Eurydice, return to darkness. Desolation is just and necessary. Revelation supersedes *poiesis*. Now the disciple must graduate to a higher teaching, to "nostra maggior musa" which is that of holy writ.

Today, only the classicist and medievalist know of Statius. For Dante and his contemporaries this first-century epic poet came just after Virgil and Ovid but ahead of Lucan in the canon. His *Thebaid* and *Achilleid* had transmitted to the west the matter of Thebes and of Troy. Cato achieved salvation because he had sacrificed himself for others; the emperor Trajan (Traiano) had been "prayed" out of Limbo by Pope Gregory for the justice of his rule. Among the Trojans, begetters of Rome, Ripheus had been "the most just." Why Dante elects Statius for baptism remains contentious and unclear. Statius himself, in *Purgatorio,* ascribes to a verse in the *Aeneid* his repentance, his inward rebirth. The Fourth Eclogue draws him towards Christ: "Per te poeta fui, per te cristiano." Poetics and faith conjoin: "before I had led the Greeks to the rivers of Thebes in my verse, I received baptism." But fear of Domitian persecution caused Statius to conceal his beliefs. Hence his laboured ascent of the Mount of Purgatory.

The start of *Purgatorio* XXI sees Master and disciple in facsimile of the Apostles on their way to Emmaus. In turn, the shade of Statius is emblematic of the person of Christ. Hence his liturgical salute: "O frati miei, Dio vi dea pace." Though it is not without an aura of irony, Gustave Courbet's *La Rencontre* reproduces the shy immensity of the moment. With mournful courtesy, Virgil identifies himself as one "relegated" from that "peace which passes understanding." For his part, Statius will do reverence to the Master, crowding his discourse with reminiscences of the *Aeneid.* The Pilgrim has taken pride in revealing to Statius the identity of his guide. In literary terms, Dante considers both Statius and himself to be Virgil's assiduous pupils. He puts in Statius's mouth a summary definition of Virgil's art. Here is a poet "trattando l'ombre come cosa salda." To give substance to shadow. This is, obviously, Dante's own unsurpassed craft.

Though Virgil is theologically doomed, the meeting with Statius, at the threshold of parting, once more exalts his poetic-prophetic eminence. The Master helps his disciples towards that light which is barred to him. Tradition had it that Statius was already a clandestine Christian when he composed the last three books of his *Theibaid.* Poetically this turgid epic cannot compare with the *Aeneid.* But in the syllabus of salvation, of the schooling of the human soul, it exceeds it. The presence of Statius will be second only to that of Beatrice on the journey to revelation.

Had one to choose one text which more than any other crystallizes the theme of this book, it would be the fifteenth canto of Dante's *Inferno.* The meeting between the Pilgrim and Brunetto Latini has been compendiously dissected and debated. Yet essentials remain unresolved. In what sense did Dante regard himself as the disciple of the Florentine diplomat, grammarian, and rhetorician? What sin accounts for Brunetto's tortured consignment to the "rain of fire"? One eminent French scholar has spent years arguing that it was Brunetto's crime to have published in French rather than Tuscan or even Latin his *Li Livres du Trésor.* This suggestion strikes me as exemplary of the academic mind after dark.

Yet the clues are insistent. And Boccaccio's later commentary, *pedagogus ergo sodomiticus,* throws crude light on a persistent motif: that of the homoerotic bonds between Masters and disciples, between teachers and pupils. The Veronese footrace, the *palio* in which Brunetto takes undefeated part was distinctly associated with male beauty and homosexual exhibitionism as was the green cloth flourished by the winner. But whatever Brunetto's sin, the Pilgrim approaches him with ardent esteem. *Siete voi* and *ser* are explicitly honorific. The disciple bends his head towards *lo mio maestro.* For it was from him that he received the quintessential lesson:

> ad ora ad ora
> m'insegnavate come l'uom s'etterna.

Supreme simplicity is untranslatable. Seven words in which Dante compacts and defines *paideia.* In which he tells us what the purpose of true teaching is and what is the aim of art, of philosophy, of speculative thought. For all time. The crux is *s'etterna.* Eliot Norton: "you taught me how man makes himself eternal." This is indeed the standard rendition. It misses the thrust, the unfolding of the original. French allows the verb *s'éterniser.* Great teaching, the education of the human spirit towards aesthetic, philosophic, intellectual pursuits "eternalises" not only the individual but mankind. Fortunate the disciple whose Master has given to mortality its sense. But vainglory would be out of place. Brunetto's shade is surrounded by a throng of "eminent clerics and of literary men of high fame." Theirs has been that "treason of the clerics" to which I will return.

The magic of the close is a touchstone. Running into the fiery murk, *Ser* Brunetto looks victorious still: "non colui che perde"—"not as one who loses." The "eternity" of poetic, scholarly discourse flares up in that other eternity of damnation. At what depths are these two connected? Dante to Brunetto; Prospero to Ariel (there is, as T. S. Eliot ruled, "no third"):

> My Ariel—chick,
> That is thy charge: then to the elements
> Be free, and fare thou well . . .

◇◇◇

Fernando Pessoa was at home with ghosts. Their busy discretion throngs his spectral Lisbon. Like Dante, Pessoa gave shadows specific gravity. From this stems the logic of his fourfold self-scission. The four poets whom Pessoa conjures into being have their perfectly distinct voices, ideologies, rhetorical manners. Their apparitions comport imagined biographies and bibliographies. They interrelate in a cat's cradle of mutual notice, suspicion or affinity through which Pessoa moves, a "secret sharer" in "exile from himself." Heteronymity goes far beyond the trope of the pseudonymous. In Alvaro de Campos, Ricardo Reis, Alberto Caeiro, and the "Pessoa" who is and is not Fernando Pessoa ("Borges and I" in the most eminent of his heirs), genius is drawn and quartered, a jugglery at once joyous and melancholy. The masks lie under the skin. Throughout this alchemy, unique in literature, Mastery and discipleship are prominent.

Reis and Campos, antipathetic to each other, both proclaim themselves Caeiro's disciples. Over some two decades, Pessoa planned to publish Caeiro's collected poems, to be prefaced by Ricardo Reis—the later protagonist of José Sara-

mago's finest novel, itself a triple mirroring of Pessoa's invention. The book would conclude with Campos's *Notes for the
Memory of My Master Caeiro.* One I. I. Crosse, translator and
essayist, was to launch in the English-speaking world this
new Lisbon school of poetry, sole begetter Pessoa.

Campos's initial, chance encounter with Caeiro proved to
be what German calls *eine Sternstunde,* "a stellar hour." The
Platonic tenor shines through. Caeiro exhibits "a strange
Greek air, which was a calmness from within . . . Those blue
eyes couldn't stop gazing . . . The expression of his mouth,
which was the last thing one noticed, as if speaking were less
than existing for this man, consisted of the kind of smile we
ascribe in poetry to beautiful inanimate things, merely because they please us—flowers, sprawling fields, sunlit waters.
A smile for existing, not for talking to us." But sorrow im-
pends: "My master, my master, who died so young! I see him
again in this mere shadow that's me, in the memory that my
dead self retains." Hearing the Master's first dictum—"Everything is different from us, and that's why everything exists"—
the disciple experiences "a seismic shock." He is seduced, but
this seduction affords his sensations "a virginity I'd never
had" (the hybrid of mystique and irony is Pessoa's hallmark).

Caeiro breathes an untroubled paganism. At times, his disciple records the physical sensation of "arguing not with another man but with another universe." To himself, the Master is nothing more "than one of my sensations." The disciple
will never overcome "the shock that phrase produced in my
soul." None the less, he takes it to be a shaft of sunlight
which illumines without any intention. Fernando Pessoa,
who lives more in ideas than in himself, participates in the
conversazione. In vain, he seeks to categorize Caeiro's agnostic

objectivism as a kind of personal Kantianism. His efforts go
to the heart of discipleship:

> This conversation remained imprinted on my soul, and
> I've reproduced it with what I think is near-stenographic pre-
> cision, albeit without stenography. I have a sharp and vivid
> memory, which is characteristic of certain types of madness.
> And this conversation had an important outcome. It was, in
> itself, inconsequential like all conversations, and it would be
> easy to prove, by applying strict logic, that only those who
> held their peace didn't contradict themselves. In Caiero's
> always stimulating affirmations and replies, a philosophical
> mind would be able to identify conflicting systems of
> thoughts. But although I concede this, I don't believe there is
> any conflict. My master Caeiro was surely right, even on
> those points where he was wrong.   (tr. Richard Zenith)

Campos's profession of faith entails the insight that "the
physical privilege of keeping company" with a Master-spirit is
not granted to everyone. Only the privileged can journey to
Rome knowing it will leave them transformed. "Inferior people cannot have a master, since they have nothing for a master
to be a master of." The capacity to be hypnotized distin-
guishes strong personalities. These retain their transmuted
individuality after passing through the sive of the Master's in-
tervention. Each case is particular: via Caeiro, Ricardo Reis
becomes "organically a poet," a metamorphosis which allows
him to change gender! António Mora, "indecisive like all
strong minds," acquires a soul. He produces, in Caeiro's hidden wake, marvels of originality and speculative thought. For
Alvaro de Campos, the encounter has proved seminal: "And
from then on, for better or worse, I have been I."

The most unsettling is Pessoa on "Pessoa." Having met

Caeiro on 8th March 1914, having heard him recite his own verse, "Pessoa" rushes home to compose six poems at one go. The fever which possesses him is exactly "the one he was born with" (there is an entire anatomy of creation in that remark). Yet the work is undoubtedly a result of the spiritual shock he underwent mere moments after meeting, hearing the Master. The enigma of autonomy within discipleship produces excellence generated by Caeiro but wholly "Pessoa's." Thus "this veritable photograph of a soul" is also an unfathomable facsimile of discipleship. "Long live my master Caeiro!"

The satire is reticent and pervasive. Pessoa was steeped in the mystery cults—astral, theosophic, neo-pagan, kabbalistic, rosicrucian—which mushroomed at the turn of the century. Like Yeats, Stefan George, Georges Bataille, the Surrealists, he felt drawn to the covens of the esoteric. But he maintained a wry distrust of his own fascination. The famous sad smile narked at himself. What aches in this magician of solitude is a thirst for dialogue, for shared risks of sensibility and intellect along Socratic lines. Hence the penetrative tenderness, the ironized pathos of the diagnoses of Mastery and discipleship. Fernando Pessoa will revert to these in his monumental *Faust*.

◇◇◇

Ateliers, workshops, master classes are instrumental throughout the history of music and the arts. They date back to antiquity and have bred their own secondary iconography and legend. Paintings, etchings, often satirical, of life classes, of composition classes in the academy and conservatory abound. Balzac, Zola, Du Maurier, Thomas Mann treat this theme. Far more classic art than we sometimes realise is collective; many hands have assisted the Master. The comedy of apprenticeship and choral drill is sparkling in Berlioz's *Cellini*

and Wagner's *Meistersinger.* All the elements we are looking to—ecstatic fidelity, mutual rivalry, subversion, and betrayal—lie to hand.

The case of literature is less clear. Rhetoric, the techniques
of poetic composition and presentation are taught throughout the ancient world. Pedagogues of eloquence flourish in
Rome, in Alexandria, in the Spain of Seneca. In Byzantium,
literature is learned, signifying "learnt." But the parallel with
the atelier of the painter or the class in musical composition
is not exact. The components of imagination, the disciplines
of articulate feeling which translate into a literary text are
rarely, or only late in literary history, formalized. Processes
of didactic guidance, of exemplary counsel, are contingent.
They arise out of charisma and a more or less professional milieu: the "tribe" of Ben Jonson, Dryden's helpful sovereignty
in the coffeehouse, Dr. Johnson magisterial at the Club,
Mallarmé at tea. Actual instruction is difficult to document.
Verifiable material dates from the later nineteenth century.
Magisterium in literary creation surfaces formidably with
Flaubert's adoption in spirit of the young Maupassant.

Maupassant's apprenticeship coincides with Flaubert's
struggles against solitude and depression after the catastrophe of 1871. Under Flaubert's tutorship, Maupassant turns to
prose. Maupassant has testified to the intensity of his discipleship during the mid-1870s. "The master read everything"
that the disciple submitted to him. He criticised in detail.
Minutiae alternated with presiding ideals: "Even the slightest
thing contains a little that is unknown. We must find it. To
describe a blazing fire or a tree in a plain, we must remain before that fire or that tree until they no longer resemble for us
any other tree or any other fire." No two grains of sand are
identical. "Whatever you want to say, there is only one word

that will express it, one verb to make it move, one adjective to qualify it." Style, taught Flaubert, is infinite specificity. On 23rd July 1876: "A man who has set himself up to be an artist no longer has the right to live like other people." The syllabus designed by Flaubert, "irréprochable Maître," was, as Francis Steegmuller put it, "a hot-house, a forcing-bed, for genius." Reciprocally, Flaubert enlisted his disciple's assistance when labouring on the ironized topography of *Bouvard et Pécuchet.*

They had met in September 1867. The epiphany came shortly before Flaubert's sudden death. It is one of the noon moments in our study. Maupassant had sent *Boule de suif.* Flaubert's recognition was instantaneous: "Cela est d'un maître." And in the midst of a sentence, unconsciously no doubt, the grant of intimate parity, the "tu" never before accorded. Consecration is emphatic: "Non! vraiment, je suis content!" As if in intimation of his nearing end, Flaubert hands on the baton: "Tu as raison de m'aimer, car ton vieux te chérit"—"You are right to love me, because your old man cherishes you." Writing to Turgeniev on 25th May 1880, shortly after Flaubert's death, Maupassant tells of the Master's incessant presence, of a voice which cannot be muted.

Flaubert's uncompromising *maîtrise* was the acknowledged icon in the tutorials which Ezra Pound—"his Penelope was Flaubert"—gave to T. S. Eliot and which Hemingway experienced, though briefly, at the hands of Gertrude Stein. But it took the American faith in the rights of all to be gifted, in the teachability of inspiration, to turn these individual acts of instruction into the institutional. It was during the late 1930s that Paul Engle initiated his Writers' Workshop at the University of Iowa. "Creative Writing" classes, seminars, summer schools, home study programmes are now an international industry, although Anglo-American dominance continues.

The questions raised are more intractable than is sometimes allowed. What would "non-creative writing" be? Does the shared attempt to produce worthwhile poetry or fiction or drama have a natural place in academic studies? Auden was among the first to warn of possible deleterious effects on the independence of the instructor, on the inevitable artifice of the situation, formally and psychologically. The measurable, "examinable" criteria of a piece of art or of music do not correspond, or only in the most superficial sense, to those in writing. At their most honest, creative writing classes are alleviations of solitude, chances to hear oneself in other voices. Tactics of potential publication, an introduction to the market, can be imparted.

Inevitably, creative writing classes have generated their own parasitic genre. The disorder of "political correctness" can provide a sombre or hysterical lining. No pedagogy is more charged with erotic potential than that between the campus bard and his flock. There is unavoidable nakedness in the submission of one's intimate imaginings to the critic's voyeuristic scrutiny. How can sexuality, now trivialized to "sexual harassment," its political-parodistic mode, be excluded? Alcibiades towards Socrates, Heloise to Abelard, Michelangelo to Cavalieri, Hannah Arendt in relation to Heidegger. Philip Roth's *The Dying Animal* (2001) displays the caustic verve characteristic of his Americana. Finally, perhaps, didacticism is every writer's destiny. The homoeroticism in E. M. Forster's "only connect" was more prudent, but no less implicit. In Joyce Carol Oates's "The Instructor" (2001) the bond grows murderous.

How far we have come from the *cortesia* of *Ser* Brunetto.

3

MAGNIFICUS

⬦ ⬦ ⬦

CHRISTOPHER MARLOWE's iambic pulse electrifies abstraction. Faustus's theological and metaphysical propositions have no less nervous thrust than the ravings of empire of Tamburlaine or the crazed vindictiveness of Barrabas the Jew. Marlowe's incandescent intellectuality spellbound his contemporaries. He had "in him those brave translunary things" said Michael Drayton. Long after, Coleridge judges him to have been "the most *thoughtful* and philosophic mind" among Elizabethan dramatists. Marlowe remains, with Milton and George Eliot, the most academic of our great writers, the most at home in the arcane glow of learning. He had spent six and a half years at Cambridge, during a decade of vehement theological and epistemological controversy. Citation was second nature to his art. The opening monologue in *Dr. Faustus* quotes Aristotle, Justinian, St. Jerome. Friar Bacon and Albertus Magnus follow. With searing irony, a line out of Ovid's *Amores* defines Faustus's horror at the passage of time. His epitaph derives from Thomas Churchyard's poem "Shore's Wife": "And bent the wand that might have grown full straight." Marlowe is as fine a hellenist as Shelley, but more expert than was Shelley in the sonorities of Augustan and patristic Latin. His astronomical equivocations, as between the Ptolemaic and the Copernican, are of the subtlest. The allusive cunning, the cerebral flash of his rhetoric and aphorisms were legend. The physical charge within speculative, technical discourse remains, almost uniquely, his. Donne is of a comparable but drier tinder.

The moment was privileged. Late medieval mappings of the world were dynamic still within the renaissance prologue to modernity. No period exceeds the late sixteenth and early seventeenth centuries in the "coincidence of opposites," in dialectical tension. Faith and reformation brush up against more or less clandestine atheism (Marlowe belongs to Ralegh's School of Night, "schola frequens de atheismo"); astrology is interleaved with astronomy; geomancy with the beginnings of mineralogy; alchemy breeds chemistry; the study of mirrors and magnets is inseparable from necromancy; the gray which lies between white and black magic is a testing ground; hermeticism and Kabbalah inspire mathematical research. How is one to dissociate the esoteric from the systematic and scientific in John Dee, in Thomas Harriot who was known as Master of Ralegh's coven?

These tensions set alight the universities. Consider the iconography of the lecture hall, of the seminar in the museum of medieval art in Bologna. The drama and *commedia* of the academic are palpable, also in the depiction of students falling asleep during the lesson. Giordano Bruno, Shakespeare's Hamlet, Marlowe's Faustus attend Wittenberg (as did Luther). Copernicus and Faustus share a courtyard, still extant, in the Jagellonian University at Krakow. Graduate study persists after death: "My ghost be with the old philosophers!"

Overreaching, titanic challenges to the gods, attempts, even violent, to appropriate the secret forces of nature, such as wind and fire, were a classical legacy. Faustus enlists conventional icons when he invokes Prometheus and Icarus. Equally prevalent, and underscored by Calvinism, was the axiom that an unbridled lust (dare one say "lechery"?) for knowledge, *libido sciendi,* had brought on the Adamic fall. The tree of knowledge had borne poisoned fruit. What was profoundly new was the intuition that an ineradicable sorrow attaches to even the most illustrious, morally defensible, acquisition of knowledge. As often, the key move was Giordano Bruno's. In his *Oratio valedictoria* addressed to Wittenberg (1588?), Bruno chooses as his motto Ecclesiastes 1:18 (the role of Ecclesiastes as the primer of the new mood remains to be studied): "who increases wisdom, increases sorrow." This anti-Platonic, counter-humanistic *tristitia* was to be resisted. George Chapman's riddling *Hymnus in Noctem,* possibly influenced by Plotinus, bids his aspiring soul "in my tortures she all earth's may sing." But the discovery of the tragic tenor of theoretical, speculative inquiry, which will climax in Pascal, was irrevocable. It sprang from the clash of two infinities. "The act of the will is infinite," taught Giordano Bruno in the *Heroic Frenzies* of 1585. But so is the realm of knowledge. Neither human will nor systematic exploration can attain the final mysteries or any complete grasp of natural phenomena. Frustration is inscribed in reason. Hence, as M. C. Bradbrook puts it, the grim paradox whereby Faustus achieves certitude only in his damnation.

The nebula of legend which expands with uncanny speed between 1507 and the 1540s may have had a biographical core: one Johannes Fust, associated with the novel deviltry of printing. Puppet-play versions multiplied across Germany and central Europe. The *Historia von D. Johann Fausten* is on sale in Frankfurt in 1587. Spiess's *Urfaustbuch* was rendered into English, together with all manner of elaborations. There are gaps in the sequence, but it would be characteristic of Marlowe's mercurial alertness to have taken immediate note. His play, of which we have two textually problematic versions, was almost certainly in existence by early 1589. Scholars contest the authorship of the farcical subplot and prose. Thomas Nashe, Samuel Rowley? It was Marlowe, as Goethe admiringly observed, who perceived the immensity of the theme and its psychological-dramatic potential. Here was a tragedy of the human spirit, a drama, even melodrama, of the intellect. Satires on pedantry and mandarin pretentions had been numerous from Aristophanes and Lucian to Rabelais. They take on a bitter edge in Bruno. Witchcraft and the occult had featured in plays, ballads, and chapbooks. Marlowe composes a passion play of the mind, a metaphysical thriller as taut and unnerving as any in Dostoevski. How un-Shakespearean is his invention and how stilted a figure is Prospero when set beside Faustus.

Sorcerers have apprentices, Masters have disciples, an *Ordinarius* or professor will have assistants. The pairing, with its prodigal occasions for parody and counterpoint, inheres in the academic hierarchy as it does in the alchemist's laboratory. Where there is a *Magister,* a *famulus* hovers (the term "familiar" connotes both intimacy and daemonic service). The agonies of Faust are inseparable from the role of Wagner even where it is slapstick. It may be that Marlowe's Wagner spoke the prologue and acted as chorus.

The academic props are in place. Troubled by rumours of Faustus's dabbling in "damned art," his "Schollers" will seek out the Rector of the University. The Master calls on Mephistopheles; in farcical parallel, Wagner threatens to conjure up minor devils. For he too aspires to the title "Maister" and would be supernaturally attended upon. Faustus's relation to his disciples is one of sovereign largesse. He allows them to glimpse incomparable Helen "when sir Paris crost the seas with her." It is in the company of his scholars that Faustus confronts his midnight. Was Faustus's "Ah Gentlemen!" the inspiration for Charmian's "Ah, soldier" in *Antony and Cleopatra*? Marlowe hints at loving intimacy: "Ah my sweete chamber-fellow! had I lived with thee . . ." As so often in his idiom, homoerotic eros and intellect conjoin. Sinning against the Holy Ghost, the Master expounds his hopeless theology. The Serpent may be forgiven, but not Faustus. A doomed arrogance and sense of fair play hammers between the lines: would the God whom he has abjured be a just God if he now forgave Faustus, would such pardon exceed His powers? (Certain divines and scholastics considered God the Father to be *incapable* of forgiving Judas.) The density of theological-metaphysical implications, with their Augustinian stress on sin as darkness in the soul, has no match in English drama.

Nor does the valediction. Faustus to his pupils: "Talke not of me, but save yourselves and depart." There is humane concern in this injunction. But also embarrassment. Marlowe registers acutely the anomalous force of shame even in the face of unspeakable terror. The Master is unwilling to let his disciples witness the bestiality of his end; the literal tearing apart of his once magisterial person. There is vanity at the entrance to hell. The scholars are empowered to pray for their teacher but "what noyse soever ye heare, come not unto me, for nothing can rescue me." (Empedocles will bid his closest disciple to leave him alone at the edge of the crater.) A jaunty horror characterizes the parting: "Gentlemen farewel, if I live till morning, Ile visit you: if not, Faustus is gone to hel." The Elizabethans were gamesmen of death.

Faustus is alone with his learning. He recalls Ovid, he cites Pythagoras's comforting doctrine of metempsychosis. Pedantry is a final resource. Now it too turns to derision: "I'll burne my bookes" (Faustus is to fire as Prospero is to water). But it is not the burning of books, a scholar's suicide, which compacts the tragedy: "burned is *Apolloes* laurel bough, / That sometimes grew within this learned man." Marlowe's concision is spacious: the god of music and poetry has crowned learning and philosophic gusto. Throughout, the Master of inquisitive erudition has been close to the Muses. Wittgenstein will hazard that philosophy might best be expressed as poetry.

Of all the numerous operatic versions of the Faust material, it is Ferruccio Busoni's *Doktor Faust,* left incomplete and first performed in 1925, which comes nearest to Marlowe's demonic vision (its only rival might be Schnittke's verbatim setting of the *Historia* half a century later). Busoni was an eminent teacher whose Berlin master classes were legendary. His Faust is *Rektor Magnificus* of Wittenberg. An ominous chorus of three scholars from Krakow present him with the book of black magic. Wagner is the Master's worshipful assistant; his posture is one of unctuous humility in the approved teutonic style. A macabre irony inspires the finale. Wagner parades in the nocturnal, snowed-in street. It is now he who is *Rektor,* whom students acclaim as *Magnifizenz.* His inaugural lecture has been "incomparable": *cum perfectione!* Faust's sometime *famulus* is now Christophorus Wagnerus, possessor of academic power and wisdom. "Gratulor, gratulor, gratulor!" intone the assembled students in a parody of German academic hymns. The *Rektor* condescends. What, after all, was his predecessor other than "ein Phantast," a muddleheaded dreamer whose alleged learning was unsound? Whose life ended in deserved scandal. The music drips satisfaction and betrayal. The student's voices recede as they bid *Magnifizenz* good night.

The dying Faust enters. He recognizes the house! "There is your chair, Pedant, you take your ease and fancy your throne to be loftier than was Faust's." Mephistopheles appears in the guise of the night watchman. As the snow falls, his lantern lights the beggar-corpse of Faust: "Has this man met with some misfortune?" His tenure shall be in hell. Busoni's reading of Wagner's ascent is among the most charged in our story.

Goethe's disdain for the academic was notorious. "He who can, does. He who cannot, teaches." To which modern wags have added: "He who cannot teach, teaches in schools of education." Had Goethe not made his own sovereign contributions to virtually every discipline, from botany, zoology, mineralogy, comparative anatomy to philosophic aesthetics, from the theory of light and numismatics to statecraft? What was Kant's deserving but dusty prose compared to his? In the imbroglio over Fichte's abortive chair in Jena, Goethe had experienced at first hand the rancour, the petty violence of university disputes. He knew how sour professorial nonentities had been when faced with Schiller's radiance as lecturer and historian.

Hence the wealth of anti-academic satire, of mockeries of the teaching process throughout the two parts of *Faust.* These, moreover, are underwritten by a morphological intuition characteristic of Goethe. He sensed in the pairing of Faust and Wagner that archetype of *dédoublement* which we find also in Don Quixote and Sancho Panza, in Don Juan and Leporello, in Sherlock Holmes and Dr. Watson—a contrastive twinning mirrored in that of the tall thin man and rotund partner which the French child's parable will designate as *Fil de fer et Patapouff.* Thus the dialectic of Masters and disciples, of Rector and *famulus,* has its physique.

The choice, in denial of Platonism, is that between "life" and the disinterested (Kantian) pursuit of pure thought. Browning's "A Grammarian's Funeral" puts it memorably:

> This is our master, famous calm and dead,
>   Borne on our shoulders . . .
>
> Here's the top-peak; the multitude below
>   Live, for they can, there:
> This man decided not to Live but Know.

Having reviewed the major realms of the curriculum—philosophy, law, medicine, divinity—Faust finds them arid. Necromancy will fling open the doors of ecstatic vitality; high noon on summits which are, precisely, not those of the dessicated grammarian but of Zarathustra. Goethe's rendition of Wagner's obsequious myopia is wicked. The couplet became proverbial: "To promenade with you, Herr Doktor, / Is an honour and brings profit." The Master's celebrity, the rever-

ence lavished on him, enrapture his disciple. But Faust's aqui-
line vision eludes Wagner's grasp. The only flight *he* aspires to
is that "from book to book, from page to page." His nirvana
is a pedagogue's chamber, warmed by tenure on a winter's
night. At which point the black poodle out of hell makes his
playful entrance.

Mephistopheles appears to have read Kant's treatise on *The
Quarrel of the Faculties.* Professorially gowned in Faust's own
mantle, he receives a tremulous freshman. Which is the road
to Parnassus? First, the *Collegium Logicum* from whose web
all sciences derive. Such is the magisterial pretender's arcane
idiom, that the student's head turns like a millstone. Perhaps
law school would be preferable? Only, counsels the devil, if
one clings to one Master, to one authority amid the babble of
eminent but contradictory voices. It is medicine which leads
to the most assured rewards. And there is always metaphysics
whose divines will dictate their lectures as would the Holy
Ghost. Goethe's own credo rings out: "all theory, my friend,
is gray / And green the golden tree of life." When the student
has left, Mephistopheles reverts to his savoury style. Enough
of the cobwebs of higher learning.

In *Faust* II, the trembling novice has become an arrogant,
rebellious *Baccalaureus.* His sometime oracle now strikes him
as a moth-eaten old man. His studies have been a waste. All
rights belong to youth, to its Icarian flight and creation of
new worlds. How did Goethe, who preferred injustice to disorder, anticipate the slogans of 1968, of the Flower Children
and the New Age anarchists? Anyone older than thirty, pro-
claims the Bachelor, would do best to do away with themselves. Deference, discipleship have crumbled into dust.

It is not, however, to Wittenberg we must look for genuine

education. The Chiron episode in the second part of *Faust* is among the more enigmatic. The Centaur's flying hooves thunder through the witchery of the classical *Walpurgisnacht.* Half beast, half man, Chiron embodies wisdom when it is energy, the natural order when it branches, in dangerous beauty, into the human. Faust embraces this symbiosis of spiritual and physical might, a symbiosis which enables Chiron to apply the healing agencies of organic substances. He is "the noble Pedagogue" *par excellence.* His pupils form a constellation like no other: Chiron has taught Orpheus, Jason and the Argonauts, Hercules, Asclepius, begetter of medicine. He has borne the child Achilles on his back. Long after Goethe, Faust's salute will retain its disturbing resonance: Chiron has educated "for its glory a *Heldenvolk,*" "a nation of heroes." What scholastic "Magnificence" can be set beside the Centaur's?

Goethe's career includes an intriguing footnote. The Olympian felt aggrieved by what he took to be the malevolent neglect of his *Farbenlehre,* that mistaken but entrancing critique of Newtonian optics. A young philosopher came to offer his services. He would champion Goethe's theory and propagate its exposition. Goethe was enchanted by his disciple's brilliance and manifest devotion. He accorded him a dozen tutorials, *privatissime,* as German academic parlance has it. But the disciple began to doubt. Reexamining Goethe's explanation of the prism, he discovered its flaws. What he found himself working towards was a refutation. Goethe never forgave Arthur Schopenhauer's betrayal.

The voluminous torso of Pessoa's *Faust* adverts only once to our theme; but poignantly. "Oh Master" says the disciple to Faust when the magus confesses his horror of death. Faust regrets his indiscretion. He bids Vincent forget what he has confided in him. "I was in my soul alone with myself, / And spoke to myself while answering you." Vincent is terrified by Faust's feverish mien. He cannot comprehend Faust's revelation to him that the world is but a dream within a dream whose dreamers are also the dreamt. He perceives only dimly Faust's claims for the endangered privileges of genius. Faust promises to see his disciple later. In our text, no second meeting takes place.

No such terror impinges on the cut-glass ironies of Paul Valéry's *Mon Faust,* his last work, published posthumously in 1946. This time, the assistant is a crystalline young woman whose name, Lust, connotes both desire and merriment. The Master dictates to his *famula.* His nervous vainglory excites her devoted teasing. Mephistopheles reveals himself to a would-be disciple: "I am professor of existence." The acolyte would be as "eminent as Faust," but the prince of darkness reveals to him the incommensurability of knowledge, the "monumental edifice of the unreadable." "All these dead to be slain," laments the student. They are already dead as dust, consoles Mephistopheles. He himself is robustly illiterate: "In my time, one did not know how to read. One guessed. Thus one knew everything."

The stricken disciple confesses to Lust: "I brought Faust my faith, my hopes, my passionate desire to make him feel all the beauty which his genius had created in a young man . . . After all, was I not also one of his works?" Lust seeks to justify the Master's "mysterious tenderness." But the disciple rebels. The boundless library chills his spirit. "Faust has disappointed me, he has wounded me, reduced me to nothing."

But not all disciples will suffer defeat.

◇◇◇

What novelist would have dared invent him? Of princely Danish lineage; a classical and virtuoso modern linguist (also some Hebrew); an alchemist and astrologer; an architect and designer of intricate astronomical instruments; a peerless observer of planetary motions; the first to name and locate a nova (1572); the constructor of a model of the solar system intermediary between Ptolemy and Copernicus; a lord magnificently choleric, with a golden nose to replace the one mangled in a duel. Tycho Brahe bestrode his world like a colossus, traversing Europe from royal court to royal court, from university to university, Wittenberg included. It was in February 1600 that Emperor Rudolph's astronomer and guide to the occult took into his Bohemian castle a virtually unknown, impoverished teacher of mathematics from Graz with impaired eyesight. For his part, Johannes Kepler compared himself to "a little house dog." He was perpetually "following someone else, and imitating his thoughts and actions . . . He is malicious and bites people with his sarcasms . . . but his masters are fond of him." (Dr. Faustus's poodle?)

Entering Brahe's opulent household, Kepler hopes "not to be discouraged but to be taught." Above all, he ached for access to Tycho Brahe's observations of celestial configurations. Had he not himself noted that the intervals in the chord of C major came close to the spatial intervals between the planets in a polyhedral, ultimately Pythagorean, model of the heavens? Secretly, Kepler already harboured doubts as to his patron's "patchwork system." It may even be that Tycho, in his guarded self, shared such doubts since his quest for the diurnal parallax of Mars in 1584. The auguries were ominous.

Kepler had come in order to be a colleague. He found himself a *domesticus,* barred from Tycho's observational treasures. Fully cognizant of Kepler's mathematical abilities, Tycho sensed that his assistant was a discreet but convinced Copernican. As K. Ferguson has it in her insightful reading: he was harbouring "a changeling with enormous mental capacities." Contrary to his own inclinations, Kepler was committed to a physical and geometric explanation of planetary motion. Both men were on the edge of paranoia. In the fall of 1601, in one of the more fraught moments in intellectual history, Tycho entrusted his future destiny into Kepler's impatient hands. The Master opened up to his *famulus* the jealously guarded horde of his astronomical tables. Who but Kepler could bring the Tychonian model to fruition? Soon Tycho lay dying. In agony, knowing that thirty-eight years of exhausting computation were now out of his hands, Tycho Brahe adjured over and over: "Let me not seem to have lived in vain."

Johannes Kepler was now Imperial Mathematician. Secretly, he retained for his own use Tycho's observations of Mars. The monumental *Astronomia nova* followed in 1609. Its preface, by Tycho's loyal amanuensis Tengnagel still advocates the Tychonian system. In fact, Kepler had swept it away. The future lay with Copernicus, Kepler, and Galileo. Yet much in his work, notably in the *Ephemeris,* continued to be based on Tycho's star catalogue. Both Master and "disciple" deserved the epitaph Kepler had composed for himself: "I measured the heavens."

This drama, enacted in and near Prague, exercised Max Brod. His *Tycho Brahes Weg Zu Gott* (*Tycho Brahe's Way to God*) of 1916 is a prolix but moving fiction. "X-rayed," it provides a document unlike any other. Official wisdom has it that Brod's novel tells of his relationship with Franz Werfel. This is, I believe, to overlook the obvious.

Brod's friendship with Kafka began in 1903. In his autobiography of 1960, which no doubt needs to be handled with care, Brod testifies to "daily contact" virtually to the moment of Kafka's death in June of 1924. "The contrasts between us were strong. Of corresponding strength was the collision of both souls." Indefatigably, Brod and Kafka read philosophy (Plato) and literature (Flaubert) together. Above all, they read each other, occasionally in public. It is to Kafka that Brod dedicates his *Tycho Brahe.* His last novel, *Mira,* will revert to an obsessive theme: that of the victorious double, of the secret sharer who destroys his twin. The ambivalent generosity in Brod's memoirs is transparent: "Where Kafka appears he dominates, owing as much to his advantages as to his weaknesses." Uniquely, his is a being which "can do no injustice, not even to objects." But on the intellectual and literary plane, their intimacy is one of equals, of mutual benefit: "We taught each other."

The deep-lying intentionality, the exact phrasing of the dying Kafka's instructions to Brod remain contentious. The mist of legend is dense. We shall never know beyond doubt. It does, however, seem established that Brod would have been at liberty, if not indeed fully authorized and enjoined, to destroy Kafka's unpublished, incomplete novels and stories. Of these a mere handful of fragments had appeared in Kafka's lifetime. We have Kafka—pause for a moment to imagine our times and modernity without him!—because of Brod's tireless labours to put in order, to edit, to find publishers for Kafka's works and diaries. Has any other act of posthumous rescue been as significant? It is, at once, an act of supreme morality and self-destruction. Max Brod *must* have known what Kafka's impact would do to his own work. A cruel anecdote survives: Brod in tears, on a rainy night, in the street of the goldsmiths and alchemists beneath Prague's castle. He meets a well-known bookdealer: "Why are you weeping, Max?" "I have just received news of Franz Kafka's death." "Oh, I am sorry. I know of your esteem for the young man." "You don't understand. He bids me burn his manuscripts." "Then you are honour-bound to do so." "You don't understand. Franz was one of the greatest writers in the German language." A moment's silence: "Max, I have the solution. Why don't you burn your own books instead?"

When Robert Bridges, lofty laureate, saw Gerard Manley Hopkins's eccentric poems through the press, he felt that he was performing a deed of inconsequential benevolence. The Brod–Kafka case is overwhelmingly different. Prior to his own death, Brod had seen himself made a respectable, largely unread adjunct to Kafka. Yet to the very end, he laboured to ensure Kafka's world glory and towering legacy. "The letter K belongs to me," said Kafka with somewhat grim humour. In the Prague context, it had belonged also to Kepler. Or should we hear the chiming consonance in *Br*ahe and in *Br*od?

◇◇◇

As I near the centre of gravity of my argument, my sense of inadequacy is numbing. The stature of the protagonists beggars one's own intellectual and psychological resources. The bibliography is already difficult to survey; yet vital, possibly decisive evidence remains unavailable. Today, we are too close to, too far from the events and their desperately complicated surroundings. It is no use pretending to detachment. The historical political elements of the Edmund Husserl–Martin Heidegger relation are unavoidable. The documents, so far as we have them, are no less repellent than they are tragic. Every word, dare one say every syllable of the relevant texts—Heidegger's *Rektoratsrede,* for example—have been interpreted and overinterpreted to the point of saturation. In his *Phenomenology and Deconstruction,* Robert Cumming devotes four idiosyncratic, minutely investigative tomes to exegesis.

But it is not only the volume and polemic nature of the commentaries, of the commentaries on commentaries—there is by now a large tertiary corpus—which interposes: it is the seminal function of these commentaries and controversies in the genesis of contemporary philosophy. From Jaspers and Sartre to Levinas, Habermas and Derrida, existentialism, phenomenology (cf. Merleau-Ponty or Granel), poststructuralism and deconstruction can be read as marginalia, though formidable in their own right, to the Husserl–Heidegger encounter. Where else in the history of western philosophy— what do we mean here by "history," challenges Heidegger?— has a personal, even private context so informed models of thought? This, in the face of both Husserl's and Heidegger's anti-biographical, anti-psychological insistence on the objective, in some ways anonymous, matrix of their work. Even the most cursory, introductory look (which Heidegger would find ignoble) will get it wrong. Yet common sense ought not to be altogether bullied, as it is in the opaque jargon and almost liturgical breathlessness of so much of Gallic hermeneutics.

Unravelling Heidegger's development has become a cottage industry. Transcriptions of lectures and seminars for the crucial semesters from 1919 to 1927 only gradually became accessible. As is, publication is not yet exhaustive. Heidegger's own subsequent accounts of the paths which led to *Sein und Zeit,* those forest tracks which led to the "clearing," need to be read with utmost caution. Even what seems plainest can best be regarded as provisional. We now know of the formative weight of the young Heidegger's immersion in scholastic theology and Thomism. Much about his turn to Luther and to St. Paul as Luther's radical subtext remains sketchy. The change of direction, the abandonment of theological for philosophic studies and the adoption of Protestantism were momentous but somehow masked. The earlier scholasticism left a pervasive "metatheological" component and style in the entirety of Heidegger's ontology. Theological classics, St. Augustine on time, Kierkegaard on "fear and trembling," were to generate fundamental moves in Heidegger's teaching. They are inwoven in what Heidegger chose to identify as the source of his lifelong philosophic focus: Brentano's treatise on the several significations of "to be," of the existential. If Brentano led him to an absolutely decisive revaluation of Aristotle, so did the Aristotelian primacy in scholasticism.

What even the most detailed, word-by-word examination of the early Heidegger by readers such as T. Kisiel, Jean Beaufret, and Cumming does *not* resolve is the crux: it is the nascence and deployment of Martin Heidegger's language. Almost from the outset, and it is that "almost" which calls for precise determination, Heidegger's idiom, his syntax, his neologisms, his "translations" from the Greek, the tidal repetitiveness of his rhetoric—and it is a rhetoric—leap at one. There may be affinities with German expressionism and the apocalyptic voices of the decade immediately following on the collapse of 1918. Compare the first version of Karl Barth's commentary on Letter to the Romans. Spengler may hover in the margin (Heidegger lectures on Spengler in April 1920). But such possible kinship falls short of the facts. The "enormity" of Heidegger's *Sprachschöpfung,* of his "language creation," enormity in originality and dimension as well, arguably, as in monstrosity, has only one precedent (of which Heidegger was acutely conscious): that of Martin Luther. One day, perhaps, we may come to understand what tectonic shifts of consciousness, what crises in the meaning of meaning made possible, necessitated at roughly the same period *Sein und Zeit, Finnegans Wake,* and exercises in Gertrude Stein.

Heidegger came to Freiburg in the winter of 1919 as assistant to Professor Edmund Husserl, thirty years his senior. They had first met at the end of 1917. Already then, Husserl had been profoundly impressed. What Heidegger now brought with him were, I conjecture, the elements of his idiom. What witness there is to his seminars and lectures on Descartes's *Meditations,* on Augustine and Neoplatonism, on Aristotle's *De anima,* refers to the mesmeric, at times "hypnotic" effect of Heidegger's spoken discourse. He may also have internalized, even at this early date, rebellious convictions concerning the complete overhaul of German universities and the instauration of a new covenant between nation and *Geist.* He was lecturing on the nature of the university and of academic study in the summer semester of 1919.

At the same time, his opposition to the neo-Kantian orthodoxy prevalent in German philosophy, together with his devotion to Husserl's phenomenology, seemed emphatic. Throughout the early 1920s, Heidegger lectures on introductions to phenomenology, to the phenomenology of religion, to phenomenological readings of Aristotle's *Nichomachean Ethics*. Repeatedly, the young assistant explicates the Master's writings on ideas and his logical investigations. Heidegger is still directing exercises in the study of Husserl's *Logische Untersuchungen* during the winter of 1924–25.

The Master, who had lost a son in the first world war, had every reason to believe that he had found in his brilliant disciple a spiritual heir and future champion. Though a man of stoic, indeed forbidding reticence, committed as Heidegger was not to the proud traditions and magisterial modes of Germanic academicism, Husserl made no secret of his contentment. Already he sensed that his own labours, unstinting, obsessive as they were, would not suffice. Capital facets of his phenomenology, of his ambition to make of philosophy an exact science, had not yet been realised. Husserl's confidence verged on the absolute. Whatever the difficulties, his phenomeno*logical* method would establish an unassailable foundation for man's perception and comprehension of the world. It would clear the fog of theological-metaphysical presuppositions from which even Kant had not escaped. It would sweep aside that "psychologism," the assimilation of mental, cognitive acts to opaque states of consciousness which, in Husserl's credo, crippled philosophy. Incomplete, also, were his strenuous meditations on the problem of interpersonal relations. Who better than Heidegger to carry on the torch?

It is virtually impossible to encapsulate Heidegger's dissent from Husserl. Scientific, meta-mathematical ideals were alien to him ("science does not *think*"). Truth was not a logical category but a mystery in motion of disclosure within concealment (*aletheia*). Despite its claim to unconditioned, neutral acts of perception, Husserl's phenomenology fell prey to worn-out metaphysical conventions and the possibility of infinite regress. It does not address the only question Heidegger regards as worth asking: "what is Being" (*Sein/Seyn*)? It shows no awareness of that "forgetting of Being" which has undermined western thought after the brief pre-Socratic dawn and which condemned even Nietzsche to metaphysics. Husserl had no insight into the historical destiny and mission of man (*Geschick*) which attaches indissolubly to the distinction (Derrida's *différence*) between existence, the extant, and Being. He is blind to the ontological pivot of "nothingness" (*das Nicht* and Sartre's *néant*).

Rejoicing in Heidegger's seeming intimacy, Husserl can have had no inkling of these dismissals. He could not have guessed at the crude derision of himself and his works which, as early as 1923, dirty Heidegger's private letters to Karl Jaspers. Close attention to some of Heidegger's lectures after 1919 might have alerted the Master. He did observe, with a touch of sadness, the charismatic spell emanating from Heidegger's person. Husserl did take note that his own students were melting away in order to attend his assistant's classes. He may have caught wind of the rumour, spreading throughout German departments of philosophy, that one Martin Heidegger, as yet unpublished, was becoming "the secret king of thought" (Hannah Arendt's formula). Perhaps a photograph tells it all: Master and disciple on a country walk in 1921. With his broad-rimmed hat and his cane, Husserl is representative of the aging *Herr Ordinarius,* his Jewish provenance almost unmistakable. Arms tightly crossed, his garb that of a Black Forest mountaineer, the young *Assistent* seems absorbed in some commanding monologue. Heidegger does not look at Husserl who is, ever so slightly, bending towards him.

Outwardly, the relation appeared flourishing. Husserl's unstinting support leads to Heidegger's first professorial appointment in Marburg in 1923. A stellar outpost for phenomenology, thought Husserl. What there is of *Sein und Zeit*
lies ready in April 1926. Husserl harvests and publishes the
mighty torso in his *Jahrbuch für Philosophie* for 1927. It is
dedicated to him "in veneration and friendship." In the face
of opposition, Husserl fulfils his ardent wish: on his retirement in 1928, Heidegger will replace him in Freiburg. It looks
to be the zenith of their collaboration. The disciple owes to
the Master everything but his genius. Then shadows gather:
Heidegger criticizes with asperity the draft of Husserl's article
on phenomenology for the *Britannica.* Husserl now under-
takes a close reading of the leviathan. He cannot as yet believe
that it is "written against Husserl" as Heidegger confides to
Jaspers. But as we follow Husserl's marginalia and annota-
tions, the deepening shock is evident. At first, Husserl hopes
for misunderstanding. Soon, however, he comes to realise
that Heidegger has systematically denied or ignored such
key concepts as the transcendental ego and of phenomenology as a rigorous *Wissenschaft.* Unavoidably trust and intimacy cool.

Of Jewish origins, married to a Jew, emeritus Professor
Husserl is placed under interdict in 1933, though he is still allowed to give lectures abroad. We owe to this fact his frag-
mentary masterpiece on the crisis of the European mind first
presented in Prague. In the brutal circus of the Nazi takeover,
Heidegger, whose sympathies with the movement antedate
its triumph, assumes the Rectorship of the University. The
students acclaim their leader, torchlight and all. To act as
the *Führer*'s *Führer,* as Plato had striven to do in Sicily, was
Heidegger's express dream. Though the difference is, assur-

edly, that of Heidegger's stature, the scenario is precisely that of Busoni's epilogue. The new *Magnificus,* party insignia in his rustic buttonhole, lords it over his prostrate, despised Master and benefactor. No doubt, the notorious *Rektoratsrede* is a palimpsest, a manifold text whose aesopian style does articulate, at involuted levels, a pseudo-Platonic, exalted programme for higher education. It has its entrancing force. But *pace* the juggleries of derridean exegetes, Heidegger's commitment to the new regime, to the unswerving service owed the *Volk* and the dictator, is strident. Heidegger's disdain for racist and eugenic doctrines made of him what the authorities quickly labelled "a private Nazi," useless to the government. The new Rector's conduct towards non-Aryan colleagues or ideological sceptics was ugly, but in a sporadic, petty way. There was much he simply chose not to take in.

Husserl endured in macabre isolation. Stubborn gossip has it that Heidegger denied him access to the University Library. There is no good evidence for this. What is certain is that Heidegger did *nothing* to lighten his Master's condition. If the dedication of *Sein und Zeit* is suppressed, it is, as Heidegger later protested, because the book could not otherwise have been republished. The acknowledgement to Husserl in the footnote on page 38 was never cancelled. At the moment of Edmund Husserl's death in April 1938, Heidegger found himself "ill in bed." Nauseatingly, in his denazification protocol of 1945, Heidegger does express regret that he did not send the widow any letter of condolence.

Husserl's disappointment over the end of his *Seelenfreundschaft* (friendship of the soul) with his beloved disciple, at Heidegger's betrayal, philosophical and personal, was profound. Already in 1928, he fathomed the abyss: "I make no pronouncement as to his personality—it has become totally incomprehensible to me. For almost a decade, he was my closest friend: incomprehension excludes friendship—this reversal in my intellectual estimate and in my relation to his person was one of the heaviest strokes of destiny in my life." Heidegger's treason "assailed the deepest roots of my being." It makes for one of the saddest stories in the history of the mind. Postmodernist apologetics make it sadder.

◇◇◇

Hellenistic teachers welcomed women to their lectures and symposia. True to its Judaic source, Christianity barred them. None the less, the theme of the elderly Master and the young woman disciple persists. The erotic undertow is never far off. Molière satirizes Arnolphe's pedagogic designs in *L'Ecole des femmes.* Agnes has been raised in "honest and chaste ignorance." She is to be the pliant novice in his Ibsenite doll's house. He seeks malleable wax for his paternalistic hands. The curriculum goes predictably wrong. Woken by the wooing of the gallant Horace, Agnes proves all too shrewd. Arnolphe, aware of his own "sick spirit," is consigned to ridicule. As so often in Molière, a thread of sadism runs just beneath the laughter.

The Reverend Edward Casaubon's sight is failing: "I want a reader for my evenings." (The lyric vibrato in *Middlemarch* is frequently overlooked.) Casaubon may indeed be a "dried bookworm towards fifty," poignantly conscious of his death-in-life. But Dorothea—"she likes giving up" says Celia of her sister—is spellbound by Casaubon's learning and pedagogic sovereignty. He is to her a "modern Augustine." To marry him would be like "marrying Pascal." The Master starts teaching her ancient Greek "like a schoolmaster of little boys, or rather like a lover, to whom a mistress's elementary ignorance and difficulties have a touching fitness." The "guiding visions" of the revealed past may be in eclipse but there is now "the lamp of knowledge."

Chapter twenty of Book II is among the most penetrating in fiction. The Rome honeymoon alerts Dorothea to the "dream-like strangeness of her bridal life." Painting and sculpture, showing "souls in their young nudity," educate Dorothea's starved sensibility. She sees now the "brokenness" of her intercourse. The dessicated "hero of erudition" is prodigal of learned commentary. It gives her "a mental shiver." Dorothea abdicates: "I will write to your dictation, or I will copy and extract what you tell me: I can be of no other use." When the couple comes home, Celia, in an image that mocks the chronological arrogance of the psychoanalytic, perceives that there emanates from Casaubon "a kind of damp which might in due time saturate a neighbouring body." Yet Book IV closes on a note of matchless humanity. Dorothea knows that her inner rebellion, contained as it was, "has narrowly escaped hurting a lamed creature." Lameness stands in for castration long before Freud. The aura is Miltonic: like eyeless Samson, Casaubon has laboured "as in a treadmill fruitlessly." Dorothea put "her hand into her husband's, as they went along the broad corridor together." George Eliot tells us that Paradise can be lost compassionately.

Twice in the history of philosophy and of literature the Master's relation to a young woman strikes a major chord.

Peter the Venerable testifies that Heloise's renown for learning, for intellectual acumen, precedes her studies with Abelard. Abelard qualifies her as *per abundantiam litterarum suprema.* But his pedagogy, even as it turns to passion, can be harsh. The *Historia calamitatum* is unambiguous: it alludes to corporal punishment, whose sexuality must have been obvious. Lou Andreas-Salomé travesties this theme in the celebrated photograph which has her holding a whip over Nietzsche and Rée, harnessed to her cart. Heloise: "I blindly fulfilled all his commandments." With Ovid as an "intertext," desire blazed into love. Every lesson in the *trivium* of scholastic learning has its edge of ecstasy. Abelard is in his forties, his disciple is eighteen at the time of their clandestine wedding. Their union is exceptional not only in its passion but in the intellectual rank, in the theological-philosophical ambitions of its partners. Among the rare Church Fathers to direct women pupils and acolytes was St. Jerome. His epistles to Marcella will inspire both Abelard and Heloise.

After the catastrophe, it was Heloise who proved stronger and more steadfast than her beloved Master. Though their lives are now torn apart, she compels him to resume his direction of her spirit, of the community of nuns she has instituted. As a consequence, the letters, so far as we can attest to their authenticity, constitute an exchange unparalleled: in them, doctrinal-ethical analyses and arguments have pressing upon them the ache of condemned love. Surprisingly, it is Pope, among innumerable writers and artists who took up the story, who sees deepest. No less than in *Middlemarch,* there are in "Eloisa to Abelard" (1717) Miltonic echoes. Despite her vows, Eloisa has "not yet forgot myself to stone." She recalls the eros of discipleship: "From lips like those what precept fail'd to move?" The intellectual loss and that of the heart are conjoined: "Long lov'd, ador'd ideas, all adieu!"

Heidegger was steeped, as we have seen, in medieval theol-

ogy and logic. I regard it as implausible that the precedent of
Abelard and Heloise was not present to him when he embarked on his liaison with his young student Hannah Arendt
in 1925. At moments, the correspondence, which will with a
grim interruption extend to 1975, can be set beside its antecedent. "That you became my pupil and I your teacher is
only the circumstance of what has happened to us." February
27th, 1925, Heidegger to Hannah: "I have been struck by
the daemonic." Together, they have experienced a night of
"transfiguration" (*Verklärung*). Arendt's dissertation on the
concept of love in St. Augustine is at once a commentary
on Heidegger's exposition of Augustine's *De gratia et libero
arbitrio* and covert autobiography. The Professor felt himself
as threatened socially, academically as had Abelard. Clandes-
tinity was imperative. A lamp in the window if a tryst was
possible; a gritty hotel on the rail line, enabling Heidegger
to arrive and leave strictly on his own. "You teasing wood-
nymph" breathes the Master. A resplendent missive follows
on the need for joyous energy rather than pedantic gravity (*Ernst*) in the soul of a young scholar. Throughout the
ecstatic autumn of 1925, Heidegger guides Arendt's studies,
notably of Pauline theology and eschatology. What tutorials
these must have been! "Have you worked assiduously for
Bultmann?" (Heidegger's colleague and interlocutor in Marburg). She must read and reread Kant in preparation for
Heidegger's seminar. The Master exults in the disciple's
"dienende Freude." The phrase is difficult to translate: its
signifies a "serving joy," a joy in service. Precisely that of
Heloise.

    Arendt seems to have broken off sexual relations in January
1926. She will leave Marburg and become Jaspers's doctoral
student in order to prevent scandal. Heidegger's letter of re-

nunciation, dated January 10th, 1926, is bitter: with her departure, his pupils are a sad lot, and "the lonely, cold days will return." "I love you as on the first day," writes Heidegger in April 1928: "The way you have shown me is longer and more arduous than I thought. It requires a whole life." The Master cites Elizabeth Barrett Browning: "and if God choose / I shall but love thee better after death." Hannah Arendt sought out the disgraced Heidegger after the war. She became his indefatigable agent in the Anglo-American world, the impresario of his translations and disputed renown. At some level, she knew of his mendacity, the chill vainglory which inhibited him from acknowledging her own writings and international status. No matter: the overwhelming impact of Heidegger's teaching, his capacity "to read as no man else has ever done," kept their hold. During 1950, Heidegger wrote poetry to his beloved servant. Abelard is a superb poet; Heidegger a halting imitator of Rilke:

> Dein—aus Schmerz erblitzter
> Nähe—großgestöhntes,
> im Vertrautesten Versöhntes
> "Ja!"
> bleibt da.
>
> Und bringt als tiefgeschützter
> Schrei gestillter Wonnen
> mir zu Nacht den Schein
> der unerlöschten Sonnen
> aus dem fernsten Schrein
> darin das Eine Selbe—
> —das ins Maaß entflammte Feuer—
> sich verfremdet in das Selbe,
> im Geheuren ungeheuer.

There remains here
your "Yes"
born of lightning-lit nearness,
of intimately reconciled.

It brings to me
the deeply guarded cry
of satisfied delight.
It brings to me at night
the glow of unextinguished suns
from the far-off shrine.
In which the one and same fire
becomes strange in it sameness,
enormous in its accustomed guise.

The pulse of remembered lovemaking beats loud. The vocabulary, moreover, is that of heideggerian ontology, of his
intimacy with Sophocles ("im Geheuren ungeheuer") and
Hölderlin. Heidegger takes pride in this congruence:

Wenn Denken sich der Liebe lichtet,
hat Huld ihm Leuchten zugedichtet.

When thought becomes lit in love,
devotion and grace have added to the light.

Called "Master of Masters," Abelard drew students from
across Europe. His disciples included eminent figures such as
John of Salisbury. Tradition ascribes to him "more than five
thousand disciples, of whom fifty became bishops, cardinals
and abbots; three among them became Popes." Heidegger's
teaching inspired not only Hannah Arendt, but Karl Löwith
and Herbert Marcuse. Via Levinas, Beaufret, the existential-

ists and the deconstructionists, he came to dominate postwar philosophy in western Europe. Soon, his influence extended to the United States. It is global. There are heideggerian study centres in China and Japan. The secondary literature defies survey. The ambiguous charisma of the Master is as potent as the work itself, so often misread or impenetrable. Derrida's attempt at equilibrium is memorable: "admiration, respect, gratitude and, at the same time, profound allergy and irony; that is why he is present all the time . . . A permanent witness, he accompanies me all the time, like a phantom. He is for me a sort of watchman, a body of thought which watches over me all the time—a custodian who watches over me all the time, a body of thought by which I feel myself being watched. He is a model—against which, naturally, I also rebel, ask myself questions, ironise." A legacy of the magisterial underlies Derrida's remarks. How, indeed, do "they order these matters in France"?

4

MAÎTRES À PENSER

❖   ❖   ❖

THE VERY PHRASE "Maîtres à penser" confines us to what Henry James called "the golden cage of the untranslatable." Not because of any semantic difficulty. But by virtue of ridicule. In the English language, "Master of thought" rings pompous and vacuous. It strikes what is to Anglo-American ears a characteristic note of Gallic pretentiousness and officious bombast. Even "thinker" is suspect. Henry James is apposite: he alone, in Anglo-American letters, bore the title. Bestowed initially in irony, in malice with regard to James's patrician airs and legislative dicta, "Master" became a sobriquet of more or less sincere esteem. It seemed to fit the man as it did no other.

In German, *Meister* has its place, given sanction by artists, sages, academics as diverse as Faust, Goethe, Wagner, and Hermann Hesse. "Do not despise the German Master," trumpets Hans Sachs in Wagner's apotheosis; the contrast with Bottom's use of "Masters" to his crew in a *Midsummer*

Night's Dream says it all. *Meister* has its provenance in the medieval guilds and universities. Today, it has all but faded and the rubric "Master of thought," *Denkmeister,* has never taken hold. Italian *Maestro* surfaces, fitful, vulnerable to irony, except in the sphere of musical composition and performance. *Pensiero* carries a density more than abstract; it has a scenic resonance and attaches only rarely to "Master."

In the fortunes of French philosophy, literature, science, politics, on the other hand, the designation and image are of paramount significance. From late antiquity to today (though the glow, as it were, is dimming) the appellation *Maître* is ubiquitous. It persists throughout the legal profession. I receive oral communications and letters headed, however undeservedly, "Cher Maître" and reply in kind. The manifold currency of the term extended to the relations between "doctors of the faith" and their female acolytes: François de Sales and Jeanne de Chantal, Jean-Jacques Olier and Agnès de Langeac, Bossuet and Mme Cornuau, Fénelon and Mme Guyon the quietist. These follow on the exalted *magisterium* we have seen in Heloise and Abelard. We will find it again in Simone Weil's discipleship of Alain. No other western tradition celebrates "Master of thought, thinking-Masters" comparably. Why their prepotency in France? (I use that orotund flourish deliberately.)

Any persuasive answer would amount to little less than an anatomy of the genius that is French; of a Latinity, classical and Christian, which innervates the French language and fabric of sensibility. From the Roman *imperium* in Gaul onward, this Latinity entails a pervasive acquiescence in the magisterial. As defining of the law courts as it is of the French Academy's (ineffective) claims to normative authority over vocabulary and grammar. The Roman halo is as resplendent in the *gloire* of the *ancien régime* as it is in the Napoleonic adventure. Strikingly, the adversaries of royal or imperial absolutism, such as the Jacobins, are equally immersed in the idiom and symbolism of Roman antiquity. They are Brutus to Caesar. To a degree unusual in Europe, French *civilitas* preserves its commitment to rhetoric, to forensic eloquence, to the cultivation of the oratorical long after the advent of post-Renaissance rationalism and science. Alain identifies an "ivresse du discours," an inebriation with the spoken word, in Socratic Athens. That rapture pervades French life. It is initiated in secondary schooling, orchestrated in politics (there is a distinctive *gloriosus* style in French military texts). Rhetoric survives the eclipse of the alexandrine and the lapidary couplet in French poetry. Each in his own manner, Louis Aragon and René Char are rhetoricians. Ingrained in French self-representation is a bias to the monumental, to the hierarchical, to the prescriptive which legitimizes the figure and function of the *Maître.* Hence the violence and extremism of the deconstructive, postmodernist revolt, notably in their feminist wing.

In December 1944, Pierre Boutang, philosopher, poet, pamphleteer, *condottiere* of the royalist right, addresses his Master, Charles Maurras, then incarcerated for collaboration with Vichy. He does so magnificently:

> Mon cher maître, mon maître, jamais ce beau mot n'a été plus complètement vrai que dans le rapport que j'ai à vous . . . la fidélité et la reconnaissance que je vous ai ne sont pas choses mortelles, pas plus que les idées et la lumière qui sont à leur origine. A bientôt, cependant, et à toujours.

My dear master, my master, never has the lovely word been more completely true than in the relation I have with you . . . the fidelity and gratitude I have towards you are not a mortal thing, no more than the ideas and enlightenment at their source. Till I see you soon and, none the less, for ever.

The chapter I want to consider is that after 1870. The antecedents are those of the eighteenth-century *philosophes,* of the prestige of Voltaire, Diderot, and the *Encyclopédie.* The conviction is widespread that the French Revolution had arisen from movements in political and social thought, from ideological polemics allying analytic discourse to the potential of political action. This alliance will reach deep into Russian affairs and the birth of an *intelligentsia.* Paradoxically, the Napoleonic regime, so wary of intellectual freedom and debate, consolidates the formal mastery of the intellect, the hierarchies of the pedagogic. The Empire codifies humanistic schooling and scientific training. It establishes the *grandes écoles,* the *Institut* with its several academies. These constitute an ensemble of didactic power and subordination no less influential than was that of the monastic and cathedral schools of Scholasticism. The exact uniforms worn by academicians reflected Napoleon's wishes. It is, however, two historical circumstances which inform the lessons of the Masters in what is known, famously, as *la république des professeurs.*

Humiliated in 1870–71, France found itself avid for "seriousness." It had not been teutonic hardware that prevailed, but Prussian superiority in systematic schooling and thought, both scientific and humanistic. The German *Gymnasium,* the universities after Humboldt's reforms, the standards of research and learned publication, had nurtured a cast of mind which exposed the frivolity, the amateurish haphazardness of intellectual and academic mores in the Second Empire. Military preeminence had been a logical outcome of habits of analytic rigour incarnate in Hegel (an analogous submission to Husserl and Heidegger will seduce French philosophy after 1940 and the occupation). Alexandre Dumas in 1873: "It is no longer the point to be witty, light, libertine, mocking, sceptical, and tomfooling (*folâtre*)." France must now confront "the very serious." If it fails to do so, it will perish.

In conscious imitation of the Berlin and Göttingen models, French ideals of pedagogy are systematized by Hegel's disciple Victor Cousin. Claude Bernard's experimental physiology, the chemistry of Marcelin Berthelot, with its industrial applications, strive to rival and excel theoretical and pragmatic achievements "across the Rhine." Zola's novels convey both the shock of the debacle and the new sociological, "physiological" methods and gravity appropriate also to literature. The two dominant voices, the Masters of rebirth, will be Ernest Renan and Hippolyte Taine. Schooled in comparative linguistics and biblical exegesis as these had flourished in Germany, bitterly opposed to the inroads of the irrational, notably Roman Catholic, into French practises, Ernest Renan makes of "let us be serious" the shibboleth of secondary and higher education. Himself a compendious exegete and historian of religion, Renan perceives acutely the decisive future of the pure and applied sciences. As his allegoric variation on *The Tempest* shows, Renan saw himself as Prospero educating the nation. Hippolyte Taine's style was that of the methodologist and social critic. The influence of his essentially materialist approach on school teaching, on the systematic study of historical and economic documents, was profound. His own research had begun with republican Rome.

The second source of the French *maîtrise à penser* was the Dreyfus Affair. It is this fratricidal drama which gives to the noun "an intellectual" and to its ancillary, *un clerc*—a cleric in the layity—their modern meaning and diffusion. The professors, mandarins, publicists, politicians in both camps pour out a periodical tide which ranges from the patriotic conservatism of the *Revue des deux mondes* to Charles Péguy's pro-Dreyfus *Cahiers de la quinzaine* and the young Proust's *Revue blanche.* The two sides produce their magisterial spokesmen: Jean Jaurès and his acolytes at the Ecole Normale, Zola, Léon Blum, Charles Maurras. Riots occur in the Sorbonne and throughout the Latin Quarter. Every intellectual institution, from the Académie and the Collège de France to provincial lycées and seminaries, is riven. The heritage of those febrile years is venomous still in the dogma of Vichy and the fury of postwar "cleansing"; "This is the vengeance of Dreyfus," cries Maurras when condemned by a denazification tribunal. France is torn between racism and universalist humanism, nationalist passion and liberalism, faith and Voltairean doubt. Polemics reach back to Plato and Montesquieu. The Ecole Normale in the Rue d'Ulm becomes that nerve centre of divisive ideologies of which Raymond Aron, Sartre, and Louis Althusser will be direct heirs. The guru at the barricades, for example Foucault, closely echoes the Dreyfus enlistment. Fiction, in Alphonse Daudet, Jules Romains, André Maurois, Louis Gilloux, seeks to communicate this feeding-frenzy of the engaged intellect. In the life of the mind, the English Channel looked oceanic.

Dumas's summons to seriousness are quoted in the preface to Paul Bourget's *Le Disciple* of 1889. The pale finesse, the "palpable design upon us" of this novel, which stands at the centre of our theme, have made of the book a relic. This is to overlook not only its contemporary impact, but also its often unnoticed legacy. Without *Le Disciple* we would not have Valéry's *Monsieur Teste.* Despite the disdain for Bourget voiced in his journals, André Gide draws on him for his sardonic studies of mastery and discipleship in his *Immoraliste,* in *Les Caves du Vatican,* and most incisively in *Les Faux-Monnayeurs.* I believe that Bourget was instrumental in Iris Murdoch's repeated fictions of sages and disciples, of teachers and pupils such as *The Flight from the Enchanter, The Bell,* and most obviously *The Philosopher's Pupil.*

Adrien Sixte—that name being the one touch of genius in Bourget's novel—enshrines pure reason as this ideal is professed by Kant. He models his daily routine on the reclusive asceticism of Spinoza. He has avoided going to mass for fifteen years, preferring the scientific materialism of Darwin. Sixte's spiritual mentor is Taine, whose "physiological psychology" guides his own thought: "The entire formula of his life was encapsulated in that one word: 'to think.'" Sixte has published a widely discussed *Psychologie de Dieu.* After which came an *Anatomy of the Will* based on the works of Darwin and Herbert Spencer. Sixte's motto is that of Monsieur Taine's notorious proposition that good and evil arise out of the fabric of the organic, that they are, in the final analysis, a matter of chemistry.

Robert Greslou enlists as his fervent disciple. House tutor in an aristocratic family, he falls in love with his nineteen-year-old charge, Charlotte. She is found poisoned. The fact is suicide, but Greslou does not seek to refute the indictment for murder. During the trial, the prosecution relates Greslou's "atrocious crime" directly to the amoral teachings of his Master. Sixte is coldly unmoved by what he regards as an absurd, vulgar association. When the disciple's desperate mother seeks out Sixte, she leaves with him Greslou's secret confession. It reveals his innocence. It demonstrates as well that Greslou's wretched fate has left intact the fervour of his discipleship. "Write to me, my dear Master, guide me. Strengthen in me the doctrine that was, that still is mine." Continue to persuade me that even this awfulness "relates to the laws of the immense universe . . . You are a great physician, a great healer of souls."

Reading this document, Sixte is shaken to the depths of his being. Thirty years of unstinting intellectual labour have carried in them "a principle of death," a poison "to all corners of the world." Can there be, asks Sixte of himself, "by virtue of a sort of mystical bond" a responsibility of a Master for his disciple's acts? Is a claim to magisterial immunity of the order of Pontius Pilate? The parable ends in propaganda. Bourget hints at Sixte's possible return to the faith. The godless materialism which brought France low will surely be routed.

◇◇◇

Though flawed, *Le Disciple* enforces one of the most arduous, intractable questions in moral philosophy and social theory. Is a Master responsible for the conduct of his disciples? If so, to what extent, in what ways (ethical, psychological, legal)? If virtue can be taught, so, presumably, can vice. Francis of Assisi imparts goodness even to fish; in *Oliver Twist,* Fagin is an exemplary pedagogue. A touch grandiloquently, Yeats asks himself whether lines in his poetry have sent to their doom "some of the men the English shot." The question lies at the heart of the trial of Socrates, of patristic denunciations of Simon Magus in the Clementine *Recognitions.* It has never lost its actuality. Bidden by their gurus to opt between Lévi-Straussian structuralism and the Marxism of the French Communist Party, a fistful of students committed suicide. From 1977 to this day, the case of Antonio Negri remains unresolved. A philosophic teacher and social critic equally versed in Spinoza and Marx, Negri gave intellectual leadership to an extreme left-wing fraction. He exercised a compelling spell over his disciples in the red brigades and *Prima Linea.* In the ferocities which ensued, these acolytes carried out acts of terror—though precise guilt is disputed. The *cattivo Maestro,* the "evil" indeed diabolical Master was charged with complicity. His had been the homicidal responsibility. A quarter of a century later, Negri is in prison still, though under mitigated conditions. The charge of incitement to murder persists.

So many factors are in play. Mastery is a salient example of the charismatic. We have seen, we shall see again, that eros, that declared or covert sexuality can permeate the power relations between Master and disciple. A desire to please the Master, to "catch his loving eye," is as manifest in the *Symposium* and the Last Supper as it is in every seminar or tutorial. Inspired coaching is an intricate hybrid of love and menace, of imitation and detachment, be it in ballet, football, or papyrology. How can one deny that the disciple's eagerness to fulfil his Master's wishes, to act in the image of the Master's ideals, can lead to praxis and enactment? "Go forth," says the Master and "the necessary murder" follows. The responsibility of the teaching, even when it is misconstrued, endures, urged Lukács, till the end of time. His consequentialist rigourism arose from the never-ending debate on Nietzsche (himself an attentive reader of Bourget). In what measure, if at all, were Nietzsche's exaltation of hardness, of a more-than-human species to come, of truths "beyond good and evil" instrumental in the rise and prevalence of Nazism? What legitimacy is there to Nazi pretentions to discipleship? Is religious fanaticism more often than not a direct fruit of the proselyte's fidelity, of the martyr's joyous obedience to the Imam?

As St. Augustine argued, a theory of pedagogy relates to the enigma of free will. It must wrestle with the proposition that God's dictates and even foreknowledge do not preclude human choice. The disciple is at liberty to discard, to revalue, to consider as merely hypothetical his Master's precepts. Innumerable Platonists have preferred to read *The Republic* and its militant eugenics as a sometimes self-ironizing utopia. *Pace* Marlowe's *Faustus,* not all "Machiavellians" behave like Caesar Borgia. In the end, responsibility does lie with the individual spirit, however influenced, however moulded. Thinking men and women are not Pavlov's dogs.

What, moreover, of misprisions? Of the numerous cases in which disciples have, knowingly or not, falsely interpreted, distorted their Masters? Is a racist, chauvinist application of Nietzschean texts, too often anthologized out of context, anything but a travesty? Is there not a vital truth to Marx's, to Freud's, to Wittgenstein's repudiation of those who professed themselves their adepts? Are the Grand Inquisitors, as Dostoevski envisaged them, justifiable disciples of Jesus? The unbroken history of the esoteric, of a Master's unwillingness to disclose his teachings to anyone but an elect handful, points to this dilemma. From Heraclitus to Wittgenstein, also in Kabbalah, Confucian ideology, or in Zen, Masters have striven to anticipate and prevent the misreading, the abuse of their doctrines. Can they be made accessories when a crazed disciple burns the temple?

To which my answer is a fumbling "Yes and No." Nietzsche's possibly sardonic invocation of "blond beasts" does not put forward a blueprint for the *Waffen SS.* But it affords it an aura of philosophic expectation. Negri's teaching that the real source of public violence is that of bourgeois capitalism, that terror is unavoidable during the struggle for a new social justice, need not enjoin the gunning down of policemen. But it provides that eventuality with a sanction of theoretically licensed inevitability. Even Jesus tells us that he came with a sword.

True teaching can be a terribly dangerous enterprise. The living Master takes into his hands that inmost of his students, the fragile and incendiary matter of their possibilities. He lays hands on what we conceive of as the soul and roots of being, a seizure of which erotic seduction is the lesser, though metaphoric, version. To teach without grave apprehension, without troubled reverence for the risks involved, is a frivolity. To do so without regard for what may be individual and social consequences is blindness. To teach greatly is to awaken doubts in the pupil, to train for dissent. It is to school the disciple for departure ("Now leave me" commands Zarathustra). A valid Master should, at the close, be alone.

◇◇◇

France had made of itself a *république des instituteurs.* Fundamental was the notion of the *laïque,* of a civic-pedagogic vocation as demanding in the secular sphere as had been that of the church and its teaching orders. Star figures in philosophy, in literature, in politics are lycée teachers during more or less extended periods in their careers: Jean Jaurès teaches, Mallarmé is a lifelong English master, Henri Bergson teaches in Angers and Clérmont-Ferrand, Simone Weil is *institutrice* to her alarmed provincial students, Jean-Paul Sartre is at the lycée in Le Havre. Rapture for the didactic can produce absurdities: in vocational classes, young women are taught the "rhetoric and poetry of housekeeping." On any given day, one half of France seemed to be setting exams and *concours* for the other.

The underlying programme and ideal were, however, of the highest kind. As Jules Lagneau proclaimed in his lycée at Vanves: "we create in broad daylight, without any concealed motive, without any mystery, a militant lay order committed to private and social duty." Explicitly or not, the model was that proposed by Fichte: culture is a branch of liberty, of moral and political freedom. This organic tie depends on schooling, on secondary schooling first and foremost. Each fully realised lesson in the classroom, however abstract or pragmatic its actual content, is a lesson in freedom. In any such lesson, as Plato reminds us, "the voice of the master is far more decisive than any book."

In the *république des instituteurs,* Emile-Auguste Chartier was sovereign. He signed himself "Alain." His was, unquestionably, a commanding presence in European moral and intellectual history. His influence permeated French education and significant elements in French politics from 1906, the year of Dreyfus's rehabilitation, to the late 1940s. Alain's prose possesses unsurpassed economy and clarity. His stoic integrity held generations of pupils and disciples spellbound. Comparison with Socrates became routine. Alain was "the sage in the city," the *Maître des maîtres.* In addition to philosophical and political writings, in addition to essays on the arts and on poetry, such as his elucidation of Valéry's *La Jeune Parque,* Alain published autobiographical reflections.

L'Histoire de mes pensées of 1936 is a jewel. As are his meditations on war in *Mars.*

Yet the very name of Alain is virtually unknown in the Anglo-American world. Hardly any of his writings have been
translated. Why should this be? I have no good answer. There
is, no doubt, a problem of context. Alain's *Propos,* the suc-
cinct but often highly wrought memoranda of which he published some five thousand in the daily or weekly press from
1906 to 1936—there is a hiatus between 1914 and 1921—touch
on "universals"; but they do so with incisive reference to the
immediate, to the political, social, ideological, or artistic occasion of the day. Alain's brevities assume shared knowledge.
For any outsider, for French readers after the second world
war and the young today, the informing circumstance has
faded. Alain's texts, moreover, were resonant with his teaching voice. With the distancing, with the disappearance of the
man, the life-giving force may have drained from the page.
Nevertheless, so much wisdom and warmth of feeling endures. Again: why the blank in British and American awareness?

For Alain, to live is to think. It is to register existence as a
boundless flow of thought. This equation had been paramount to Descartes and to Spinoza, both of whom loom
large in Alain's teaching. But neither had fully acknowledged,
let alone communicated, the "carnality" of thought, its unison with the human body and with all that is material in the
world. Alain did draw on Marx, but this "materialism of consciousness" was urgently his own. No one but Alain would
have declared that in Plato, beyond any other, there speaks "a
celestial love of earthly things." Like Socrates, Alain scruti-
nized and rejoiced in the everyday, in crafts and métier, in the

apparently innate drive towards making which relates the skill of the carpenter to that of Rembrandt or Bach. The hybrid of technical invention and intellectual analysis, in the bodily and mental substantiality of war—he refused a commission and served in the ranks during 1914–18—absorbed Alain precisely as it had Socrates. But all substance is thought; human existence is "thought in the process of becoming." Something of Alain's manner and "Platonic materialism" might be compared to Cardinal Newman's *Apologia,* to R. G. Collingwood's *Autobiography.* The Henry Adams of the *Education* would have understood Alain. But in the Anglo-American canon, these books glow solely from the margin. How can Alain's stature be valued where the very term "intellectual" comes close to being pejorative?

Alain's mentor was Jules Lagneau on whom he published his *Souvenirs concernant Jules Lagneau.* The philosophy classes taught by Lagneau in what might be called an "upper sixth form" (*première supérieure*) from 1887 to 1889 proved crucial. Lagneau's creed, expressed with no hint of mandarin ostentation—Lagneau and Alain left that to Bergson—was lapidary: "the only thing which can be fruitful is a living instruction, a teaching by and of the entire soul, of the whole person, of life." Unpublished—Socrates once more—Lagneau inspired a pedagogical-philosophical tribe. He taught his young pupils that atheism is the salt which preserves faith from corruption; that the fact that there is thought consists only in thinking. It was during these lycée sessions, whose impact he compares to that of Beethoven, that Alain adopts his Cartesian password "generosity," meaning an absolute fidelity to the freedom of the will when it is put to moral and to rational use. Empiricists such as Epicurus, Hume, John Stuart Mill, will elicit

Alain's respect; but he inherits from Lagneau an unwavering "transcendentalism," an ultimately Platonic—Plato "that author justly called divine"—idealism grounded, as we have seen, in the dignity of matter. It is from Lagneau's reading of Spinoza that Alain harvests his own definition of man's highest good: "to experience the joy of thought and to pardon God." Always, Lagneau began with a text; only to depart from it via a seemingly improvised, vividly personal, anti-systematic yet methodical commentary. This was to be Alain's style.

It took him from dim postings in Pontivy and Lorient to Rouen. Paris followed in 1903, inevitably. First at the Lycée Condorcet, Proust's alma mater, then, from 1909 onward at the Lycée Henri-IV, *primus inter pares.* The *Propos* had begun appearing three years before. Already Alain's teaching was becoming legend. "We were not attending an exposition of the ideas of Plato and Descartes," remembered one pupil, "we were in their presence. Without intermediaries." Convinced that secondary education matters more than any other, Alain refused both the Sorbonne (he gave classes there as an extramural) and the laurels of the French Academy. These abstentions by "the little Norman peasant" only heightened his stature. As France's most important publisher put it: "This great pagan, cynical, ascetic, gourmand provides us with the theme of our morning prayer." To the young André Maurois, his teacher was simply "the just one" (*le Juste*) in a corrupt and bewildered society.

Alain's impact, his almost unchallenged position as "teacher of the nation," *praeceptor galliae,* was in part owing to a contingency unavailable in the Anglo-American system. The lines between secondary schooling in its senior classes in the lycées, the "normal schools," the so-called *grandes écoles,* and the university were kept fluid. Listeners from the neighbouring Sorbonne and Ecole Normale came to hear Alain at Henri-IV. He, in turn, gave courses at the elite normal school for young women in Sèvres as well as in evening classes for working people. In the lycée his classroom spilled over. In 1928, some ninety pupils and auditors fell silent as the Master entered and wrote on the blackboard: "Happiness is a duty." Or: "It is the most beautiful law of our species that that which is not admired is forgotten." A degree of austerity and fierce privacy characterized Alain's contacts with his students. But there were gusts of affection. When Simone Weil undertook her direct actions on behalf of the unemployed, her Master noted his pleasure. She was to him "the child Simone Weil." His last class was scheduled for 1st July 1933. It was so crowded with illustrious officialdom that Alain returned once more to teach "seriously" two days later. Alluding to the disturbing pomp of the previous session, he remarked that "conditions for our study of justice and of charity were deplorable." No adieu. Grandeur has its reticence (I saw F. R. Leavis exit from his closing lecture in precisely the same fashion). Man is not merely one who lives, taught Alain in a rare moment of pride, "he is one who survives."

Alain's range was kaleidoscopic. Unison lay in his compelling voice. His pedagogic principles, moreover, did not waver. It is the shaping of the young, indeed of the child, which will determine the health of the body politic. Teaching should focus just above the pupil's reach, rousing in him or her effort and will. "I want, therefore I am," a variant on Descartes's *cogito* in which English "to want," meaning both to desire and to lack, is truer to Alain than French *je veux.* The supreme moral rule is "ne pas réussir," to abstain from success in a world in which "success" ineluctably entails compromise and an exaggeration of one's own achievements. This exigent, understated code was imparted to each of Alain's successive classes with, as one pupil has put it, "Alain's Socratic smile." Sobriety in prose is the hygiene and courtesy of the soul. The Master's nose for ostentation, be it in the composition of a student, in the sonorities of an academician or the eloquence of the so-called statesman, was acute. Yet where the act of thought was of hard-won strength, even a convoluted idiom could carry all before it. Whence Alain's memorable eulogy of the "poetry" in Hegel.

One must read and reread the Masters: Plato ("All is truth in Plato, which does not imply that one must believe all he says"), Aristotle, Montaigne, Descartes, Spinoza, Leibniz, Hegel, Comte, and Marx. To read and reread them as contemporaries, in a sense, of each other but also of ourselves. The initial reflex must be one "of reverence, of granting total credit to the author." Then comes doubt and even refutation. But these are founded on the (joyous) persuasion that our understanding of the great texts is always inadequate, that it falls short of prodigalities of significance which are dynamic, which alter as texts and contexts interrelate. There is a Plato *after* Descartes, an Aristotle in dialogue with Comte's positivism and Marx's sociology. Thus for Alain, reading is the least passive of enterprises. It empowers the orality of magisterial teaching. Literature is no less formative than philosophy; poetry probably marks the summit of man's possibilities (Plato is a supreme poet). Alain will write commentaries on Balzac, Stendhal, Dickens, and Valéry. To the extent that he had detected in the new "scientism" a betrayal of the indispensability of literature, Bourget had been right.

Each of these philosophic, didactic, and aesthetic engagements aspires to a common end: the establishment and maintenance of a *société libre.* For Alain, such a "society of freedom" must be, in the Kantian sense, a critique of human values and a self-critique. This is one of Alain's most arresting beliefs. A valid republic is a school, an examination which the will of the citizen must pass. Together with Plato and Auguste Comte, Alain is convinced that the state is or ought to be "une scolarité morale," a schooling in ethics. This is the polis of Plato's *Laws.* The splendour of republican France lay in its willingness to risk civil war, to imperil its national security in order to render justice to Dreyfus. There is in this entire creed a mixture, sometimes unstable, of cultural elitism, of Platonic "Guardianship," and of an instinctive populism, of a respect for artisan and agrarian practices. The "little Norman peasant" remained tenaciously in the *premier professeur de France.*

Alain figures in a host of memoirs; also in fiction (e.g., Roger Bésus's *Le Maître*). But *maestria,* particularly in the schoolroom, has, as Bourget argued, its tragic side.

Physically deformed, chronically ill, sexually disadvantaged, Georges Palante taught philosophy in a number of obscure Breton lycées, notably that of Saint-Brieuc. The Sorbonne declined to recognize his theses. Palante found it difficult to maintain discipline. His pupils organized what is known in French as *le chahut,* more or less systematic bouts of choral noise making and derision which rendered Palante's lessons inaudible (no *Goodbye Mr. Chips*). Enmeshed in an absurd "affair of honour," in which he thought himself patronized even by his own seconds, Palante shot himself on 5th August 1925. Yet there were those who found his teaching superlative. Palante initiated in France a Nietzscheanism of the left and was among the earliest to draw attention to Freud. A colloquium on Palante's work took place in 1990; a complete edition followed eleven years later.

Louis Guilloux became Palante's pupil in 1917. He recognized in his teacher a spirit of profound, if haunted, originality. We owe to this insight one of the masterpieces of modern French fiction: *Le Sang noir* (1935). Ridiculing his passion for Kant's *Critique of Pure Reason,* Palante's tormentors call him Monsieur Cripure. Only a handful take in the austere penetration of his teaching, the reticent magic implicit in the name of Guilloux's protagonist: M. Merlin. Pythagoras and Empedocles already knew that students can turn murderous.

The mystique of the Maître persists in the somewhat melodramatic scenario of French intellectual life. Among a coven of disciples, which includes Derrida, Gérard Granel, who taught philosophy in Bordeaux and Toulouse, has become legend. His lectures, his opaque expositions of Kant, Marx, Husserl, and Heidegger, his programme for the revolutionary transformation of the university system, circulated among adepts like revealed writ. To have been Granel's student equalled an *honoris causa.* However histrionic his behaviour, however undecipherable his writing, Jacques Lacan has commanded an almost hysterical measure of adulation and discipleship. Louis Althusser is, today, little read. His gloss on Marx has been shown to be a dogmatic eccentricity. But the persona of the guru and his macabre fate still cast their spell. As Granel put it: "although *philosophy* only deploys a series of texts within history, *thought in philosophy* belongs to an *oral* tradition." This tradition can only be transmitted from school to school, which is to say from Master to Master.

◇◇◇

Those, like Georges Palante, overwhelmed by Nietzsche, were legion. Texts, truncated, misread, mendaciously edited, acted like an avalanche. Such are Nietzsche's presence and the ambiguities which attach to it, that the derivation of western modernity from the triad Marx-Nietzsche-Freud is now a cliché. But often overlooked is the role, perhaps primary, in Nietzsche of the teacher and educator. He was the counter-academic academic *par excellence.* Only recently, with the publication of Nietzsche's juvenilia, has the voluminous philological, text-critical research amassed by Nietzsche during his student years in Bonn and Leipzig and during his professorship at the University of Basel become accessible. The erudition fills volumes. At an implausibly early age, Dr. Nietzsche is a specialist on Diogenes Laertius. He offers courses on Homer, Hesiod, Theognis, Thucydides, Aeschylus, Aristophanes, Xenophon, Plato, and Isocrates. Both at the University and the *Paedagogium.* He is a textual critic in the most demanding technical sense. At twenty-three, Nietzsche was being regarded as the most promising classicist of his generation.

In the midst, however, of these learned philological labours, wholly traditional in method, come lightning flashes of doubt and hints at rebellious innovation. Do textual recension and lexical-grammatical emendation truly reveal the ancient text? Does mandarin commentary, habitually written in Latin, serve any larger cultural, heuristic purpose? This heretical unease already smoulders in Nietzsche's *Democritea* of 1867–68. In a letter of 1868, Nietzsche uses a phrase charged with explosive connotations: "Philologie der Zukunft" (a

"philology of the future"). The tag, which will be thrown
back at Nietzsche by Wilamowitz and the classical professorial establishment, adumbrates a philology which will draw
on philosophy, which will enlist the aesthetic theories of Goethe, Schiller, and Kant. The essay of 1873 on "philosophy in
the tragic age of the Greeks" affirms Nietzsche's concordance
of Greek tragedy with music and with the ideal of the
Gesamtkunstwerk, the "total art form," as embodied in Wagner's Bayreuth.

This argument had inspired Nietzsche's first book, *The
Birth of Tragedy* (1872). It is internal contradictions between
scholarly and aesthetic criteria that yield this confused masterpiece's enduring fascination. It eludes any confident or
single-minded reading. Consciously or not, Herr Professor
Nietzsche had chosen to make himself impossible in his
guild. At the same time, in deepening isolation, Nietzsche
would seek to hammer out a pedagogy, a syllabus for future
humanity, in both the restricted (*humaniores*) and the em-
bracing sense of the term. How can we best define the true
Master?

He addresses the question in "Schopenhauer as Educator"
(1873). We are fortunate if we find "the one teacher and
Zuchtmeister"—an epithet with no equivalent in English signifying a "Master of deportment," in a sense at once intellectual and harshly behavioural. A great teacher "reshapes man
so as to become a planetary system." Academic institutions
fail to "educate a human being to become a human being"
(the echo of Dante to *Ser* Brunetto is near). To come upon
Schopenhauer is to enter a lofty forest which allows us to
breathe deeply and be restored. There inhabits teachers of
the order of Montaigne and Schopenhauer a singular "gai-

ety," that *fröhliche Wissenschaft* which will become Nietzsche's own. Schopenhauer's quest for discipleship had been frustrated; almost to the close of his life, his philosophic *magnum* had lain unread. No less than Empedocles, the author of *The World as Will and Representation* had experienced an exasperating isolation. Nietzsche will initiate true discipleship, transmuting Schopenhauer's few readers "into sons and pupils."

How does such a Master educate? By enforcing on us an upward, also transgressive motion. We recognize this performative gift when observing on the Master's countenance "a gentle evening tiredness" (*Abendmüdigkeit*). But even a Schopenhauer "finds it impossible to teach love." The corollary in Nietzsche's portrayal is a bitter critique of schooling and higher education as these are routinely practised. Academic philosophers inflict their own vacancy. If possessed of some spark, they publicize what should be revealed only to intimates. Hence the castration, the impotence of university philosophy (*Entmannung*). Hence also, Nietzsche was, after Kierkegaard, the first to see this clearly, the alliance between the academy and journalism, between thought and high gossip. So much here anticipates Wittgenstein. Schopenhauer reveals to those qualified to become his disciples that "love of truth is something terrifying and violent." In support of this axiom, Nietzsche cites one of his own rare begetters, Emerson. He also knew the perils of transforming argument.

If love cannot be taught, can hatred? In this "untimely" tract, Nietzsche provides no answer. The question is worth bearing in mind.

During the rest of his life, Nietzsche will proclaim his contempt for the university. The very short years at Basel had undermined his health. Only total independence and aloneness can generate thought of the first rank. Yet time and again, the same Nietzsche cries out that solitude is driving him mad. Anguish turns virtually unbearable after the failure of *Thus Spake Zarathustra* in 1883–85. Nietzsche's letters confess to unendurable isolation. There is not the faintest resonance to his work. When one or two far-off voices express admiration or interest (Brandes, Strindberg), Nietzsche's gratitude verges on the hysterical. A conventionally polite note from Taine, to whom Nietzsche had sent his work, elicits wild claims of recognition, of alliance. There is, in fact, only one disciple. Peter Gast, the ephemeral composer, devotes his existence to the Master. Amanuensis, literary agent, messenger, host to his suffering idol, Gast repeatedly rescues Nietzsche from suicidal despair. This was the background to Nietzsche's relationship to C. J. Burckhardt, his sometime colleague at Basel. Mutual esteem, even closeness at the start. Soon, however, the patrician cultural historian, the inward disciplinarian, flinched. He intuited in Nietzsche symptoms of chaos, of megalomania. Nietzsche's collapse found him compassionate but unsurprised. For his part, the errant prophet had striven to enlist Burckhardt's understanding, to tempt from a spirit he admired some motion of empathy, of enlightened response. His proud cries went unanswered.

The fourteen-year-old schoolboy had already arrived at an iconic programme. The archetype of the Master is that of a sage who withdraws into and then descends from the high places. His teaching gathers to it disciples, but will incite them to abandon him. Esoteric wisdom is phrased in parables. In the adolescent's project for a didactic epic, the exemplary presences are those of Empedocles and Jesus, of the Buddha and Zoroaster. Moses descends in visionary rage from Sinai:

Auf nackter Felsenklippe steh ich
Und mich umhüllt der Nacht Gewand,
Von dieser kahlen Höhe seh ich
Hienieder auf en blühend Land.
Ein Adler seh ich schweben
Und mit jugendlichen Muth
Nach den goldnen Strahlen streben
Steigen in die ewge Gluth.

I stand on naked cliffs
And draped in the cloak of night,
From this barren height
I look down on a blossoming land.
I see an eagle soar
And with youthful ardour
Rivalling the golden rays
He ascends into the eternal blaze.

Add to this the figure of Klingsor in Wagner's *Parsifal* and the epiphany which Nietzsche experienced in the Engadin, and you have the components for Zarathustra.

The idea for this "Fifth Gospel" overwhelms Nietzsche in the noonday solitude of Rapallo. It will absorb him from January 1883 to February 1885 (the first unified edition appears only in 1892 when Nietzsche inhabits his "nighttime" of madness, the *Umnachtung*). Book I blazes with promise, with the revelation to elect disciples and, thereafter, to the world at large, of the "superman" to come. Thrice, the Master will descend from his mountain cave to instruct the three (Platonic) orders of mankind: common folk, the warrior caste, and the philosopher-poets for whom Nietzsche had dreamt of a monastic *castello*. Book II is brimful of disappointment. The

Master is rejected, even derided. Seeking to unveil to his disciples the secret of "Eternal Return," of cyclical time and accepted fatality, Zarathustra fails. His voice is spent. Those whom he would teach are not "men," but mere "fragments of men."

Formally, Book III can be read as a drama inspired by Sophocles and Hölderlin. In the plague-stricken city, the disciples disperse. They are terrified by the message of "Eternal Return." Zarathustra perishes in an act of tragic violence. But Nietzsche abandoned this scenario. Instead, we have the sage's ample monologue, his "Song of the night" and return to the world of ordinary human beings. The fourth Book, printed in forty copies of which Nietzsche, aching for response, sent out seven, is a set of riddling fragments. Zarathustra terms himself a "fisher of men," with reference not only to Jesus but to the Orphic-Pythagorean model, notably Lucian's *Piscator.* He writes to his Basel colleague, Franz Overbeck: "already in my lifetime, I need disciples. If my books do not act as bait, they will have failed in their intent. The best, the essential can be communicated only *from one human being to another,* it cannot, it must not be made 'public.'" Observing his frustration, the animals with whom he converses bid Zarathustra relinquish speech. He must learn to sing, as did Socrates in the hour of his death. Ideally, Zarathustra must "dance his meaning."

As Heidegger underlines, Zarathustra is himself a *Werdender,* "one who is to come." His teachings are unstable, even contradictory. This complicates discipleship. Even as innovative art, music, literature must create its audience, so Zarathustra's doctrines must create ears capable of hearing the Master's unprecedented voice. After the death of God, only the Superman will be empowered to engage in genuine dialogue. Without solitude there is no vision; without an audience, however restricted, no truths can be revealed. But is a Master licensed to communicate with those perhaps too weak to endure his revelations, to those who, inevitably, will vulgarize and distort them? (It is as if Nietzsche foresaw the destiny of his works in Nazi hands.) Zarathustra does not resolve this dilemma, inherent in all Master-disciple situations. Particularly in Book II, he blames himself for being incapable of transmitting to his *Jüngern* his esoteric perceptions. Like Wittgenstein, he knows that authentic discipleship should end in rejection. The true disciple can only be one who "will learn to follow himself." The preeminent virtue of the Master (*die Schenkende Tugend*) consists in bestowing a gift which must be spurned. Not only shall the disciples leave Zarathustra: they will have to calumniate and deny him to the point of murder. Should the Master avoid that fate, he will return at "the great noon." Only then will Zarathustra and his disciples have become fellow celebrants and "children of one hope":

> You had not yet sought yourselves: then you found me. So do all believers; hence the triviality of all belief.
>
> Now I bid you lose me and find yourselves; and only when all of you have denied me, shall I return to you . . .
>
> And that is the great noon, when man stands midway between animal and Superman and celebrates as his highest hope the way to evening, for that is the way to a new morning.

Also Dante stands midway on his journey. Has there been, since his salute to Brunetto, any definition of teaching more inexhaustibly concise than that of becoming "children of one hope"?

◇◇◇

The *Bildungsroman,* a narrative of ripening, of inward coming of age via education and experience, is a constant in German literature. It includes classics such as *Parzival, Simplicissimus,* Goethe's *Wilhelm Meister,* Mörike's *Maler Nolten,* the *Grüne Heinrich* of Gottfried Keller, and, in a tragic mode, Mann's *Doktor Faustus.* A fascination with the pedagogic has proved perennial, also in what was East Germany. The notion of a "pedagogic eros" surfaces in Schiller's programme of aesthetic schooling and nurture. Moral, aesthetic pupillage is proclaimed in Mozart's *Magic Flute.* To these ideals or fantasies of disciplined cultivation and joyous obedience, Robert Musil's *Törless* will generate a fierce denial, and Heinrich Mann's *Blue Angel* a satyr play. To this tradition, Nietzsche's *Zarathustra* added a mesmeric if unnerving stimulus.

Short of Dante's *Commedia,* the most extended allegoric treatment of Mastery and discipleship is to be found in Hermann Hesse's *Glasperlenspiel* or *Magister Ludi* of 1943. Composed in the nighttime of European barbarism, the novel acted as a missal to postwar generations. It rang changes on the name *Meister—Weltmeister, Musikmeister, Lehrmeister—* of unprecedented, if at times saccharine, solemnity. Their sonority has not altogether faded. The theological, metaphysical, musicological, political components which Hesse enlisted and interwove, the prophetic intimations of game theory and the computer command not only respect, but an almost troubling fascination.

Hesse's "Pedagogic Province" and *paideia* have ancient

roots: in Orphism and the Platonic republic; in Tao and Confucianism; in medieval monasticism and the Neoplatonic academies of the Florentine Renaissance; in Freemasonic rites and theosophy. The glass-bead game itself incorporates the word play of the Kabbalah, a clustre of numerologies, and the discovery by E. F. Chladni, in the late eighteenth century, that when sound waves are emitted, figures will emerge in the sand strewn on a metal plate. Cosmology, as taught and "played" in Kastalia, springs from Pythagorean imaginings of a musically informed universe, imaginings still active in Kepler and in Schopenhauer. Specific antecedents can be found in that combinatorial unification of all knowledge and memory promised by Ramon Lull and Leibniz. These exact dreamers invoked Chinese characters in their programme for a universal, infinitely combinatorial semiotic code. In Hesse's utopia, such a code will be put in place by one Ignotus Basiliensis in about 2030 (a striking guess). The game enacts a "magic theatre" in which the intellect can formalize and interpret reality. The "Great Games" are lofty celebrations which can last days or even weeks, as in master play in Go. Unlimited, self-deploying reticulations of knowledge, of unsuspected patterns, are rational metaphors which knit the cosmos and guide the human mind towards the harmony of the spheres. Lest the figurations in play degenerate to literalism or ornamentation, the game is to be framed by strict practices of meditation, by techniques of self-denying concentration as taught by cloistered asceticism in the west and Zen in the east. The Kastalian knows neither women nor money. Such asceticism of spirit has made possible the fugues of Bach.

Yet the game is neither theology nor philosophy. It is simply and wholly itself. It clarifies the wise passiveness and mystery of hazard, in the manner of the I-Ching or Heidegger's ideal of *Gelassenheit*. When the young Knecht, whose name signifies service and obedience, hungers after certitude, the *Musikmeister* admonishes him: "the doctrine you desire, absolute, complete, guarantor of wisdom, does not exist . . . The divine is in *you*, not in concepts and books. Truth is lived, not taught" (where *doziert* points to the abstract and academic). Pure Spinoza. Moreover, as Zarathustra enjoined, each one of us is "merely an attempt, an 'underway.'" Nearing the summit of the Kastalian hierarchy, Josef Knecht comes to perceive its artifice and the complaisance which can inhabit its abstentions from mundanity. He who is to be consecrated Master of the Game as was Thomas von der Trave—an affectionately ironic silhouette of Thomas Mann—descends into the everyday. He becomes house tutor to a gifted boy. Knecht's death is part epiphany, part self-sacrifice. Hesse's high fable closes with an Indian parable rejoicing in the wonder of "the relation between Master and pupil."

Homoeroticism is softly pervasive in Hesse's novel. It turned histrionic in the "George Circle" (*Kreis*). Stefan George was a poet and poet-translator of undoubted stature. He incarnated the mystique of mastery, of a *magisterium mysticum*. Deeply influenced by Mallarmé, Stefan George conceived of a life form and praxis at once esoteric, even occult and of intense political implication. An "elite of the soul," chosen by the Master, secret yet also public, was to restore the cultural and moral values of a degenerate nation. Again, the Empedoclean-Platonic dream is operative. The Circle is founded in 1892, together with its periodical, *Blätter für die Kunst*. Himself of leonine handsomeness, George institutes a symbolic typography and layout for his works, using the Indian swastika as an emblem of solar illumination. His *Teppich des Lebens* declares, though in hermetic style, George's mission: to be the teacher and singing Master of the German soul. In Munich, in 1903, the rhapsode meets a fifteen-year-old acolyte in whom he sees the embodiment of perfect beauty. Maximin, who dies a year later, is idolized by George and his coven. *The Seventh Ring* (1907) hymns a new elite of youth and virile resolve which will renew a civilization "gone in the teeth," as Pound put it at almost the same date. A Germany to come, worthy of Hölderlin, is invoked in *Der Stern des Bundes* of 1911 and in *Das Neue Reich* published in 1928. Both titles soon have their menacing actuality. The Nazis sought to enlist George's oligarchic mystique. He recognized in Hitlerism a crass travesty of his apostolic leadership. *He* could have been the true *Führer*. Stefan George went into exile and died in Switzerland in late 1933.

His disciples included poets, historians, scholars, young patricians with military and diplomatic ambitions. As in the case of Heidegger, and with analogous ambiguity, the *Kreis* included Jews. Its scenic model was that of the *Symposium,* whose rites were actually performed in antique costume. We find the typology of election, fervent trust, and on occasion betrayal. George demanded prophetic authority over his disciples' private affairs. To leave the Circle was inadmissible. To be ousted from it meant "a death sentence." Some, like Hugo von Hofmannsthal, emancipated themselves. Rudolf Borchardt, a considerable poet-scholar in his own right, became a bitter adversary. Contact with the Master changed lives.

The *George-Kreis* represents, in heightened intensity, a

fairly widespread phenomenon of the late nineteenth and early twentieth centuries. One need think only of the Cambridge Apostles, of the pseudo-Rosicrucian cult around Madame Blavatsky (as shared by Yeats), of the pre-Raphaelite Brotherhood in English art, of the Gurdiev cult, in which Katherine Mansfield was enmeshed, of aspects of Bloomsbury. Why this proliferation? Aestheticism entailed a flight from the *vulgus profanum* of industrial and mass-consumption society. These diverse "cells" shared the belief, often Nietzschean in origin, that renovation could come only from an initially occult revelation and discipleship. There are marked traces of this intuition even in Shaw's peculiar socialism. Aesthetic "gurudom" probably enacts a partly subconscious riposte to the emergence of dictatorial political ideologies and *Duce* figures in Leninism, Fascism, National Socialism. The Nazis will have their *kitsch* mythology of Aryan election, of torch-lit initiation and fidelity unto death in the *Ordenburgen* of the SS.

Too much in George's Mastery now rings hollow. But it is redeemed by its tragic epilogue: the murder of a number of George's disciples who had plotted against Hitler in the summer of 1944.

The typology of elect membership, of discipleship and betrayal characterizes a movement committed to ideals of scientific inquiry, rational diagnosis, and universality. The tragicomedy of Freud's relations to his disciples goes far beyond the limits of this brief study. It has produced a secondary literature at times almost farcical in its acrid minutiae. Freud presents rings, engraved with the talismanic motif of the Sphinx, to six dauphins. Together with the Master, they constitute what George had called *Der siebente Ring.* The chosen are to safeguard the orthodoxy of the psychoanalytic creed and to perpetuate that orthodoxy after the Master's death. Fierce jealousies erupt around the theme of the "crown prince," of primacy in regard to Freud's trust and heritage. "Transferences," qualified by psychoanalysis as repressed homoeroticism, are rife. Rebellion leads Jung, Rank, Adler to create their own schools, in more or less bitter dissent from the Master. Wilhelm Reich becomes his angriest critic.

Saddened, Freud cannot have been surprised. His central reading of Oedipus comported patricide. Civilization had arisen from the murder of the father. Having identified with Moses, having perceived the fate of psychoanalysis as that of a long march through the desert, Freud must have intuited that Jung would turn out to be Aaron, that Adler would be "Judas."

In her *Flight from the Enchanter* (1956), based largely on the person of Elias Canetti, Iris Murdoch captures the anguish of discipleship. The Master becomes at moments "the very figure of evil." The "iron discretion" he would impose, the "total availability" exacted from his circle, can become insufferable. How many felt in regard to Freud what Murdoch reports of "Mischa Fox": "Always at the last moment and without apparent reason there would come the twist, the assertion of power, the hint of a complexity that was beyond her." The disciple flees or commits treason so as to rescue his or her identity from unbearable charismatic Mastery.

To cite Heine: "It is an old story, / But those who experience it have their hearts broken in two."

5

ON NATIVE GROUND

❖   ❖   ❖

A GENERALIZATION, suspect, as are all generalizations: my theme goes against the American grain. Irreverence is as American as cherry pie. The very word "Master" carries the stain of slavery. There have been, there are, great American teachers: Ralph Waldo Emerson, first and foremost, Oliver Wendell Holmes Jr., Charles Eliot Norton, John Dewey, Martha Graham. Particularly in rural America, the "school-marm" enters folklore and legend. But the context of formalities, the explicit clerisy and *magisterium* inherent in European culture, the social prestige of the intellect outside any economic reward are, at best, marginal to the American enterprise. Which is one of Adamic innocence and discovery, of talent not doctrinally schooled (*doziert*) but self-made. What elite secondary education there is (or has been) in imitation of the English "public school" accords uncomfortably with a commitment to the egalitarian, to a populist ideal of social justice. The mythology, the public role of the *Gymnasium,* of the *grandes écoles*—what good did they do strife-torn, then barbarized Europe?—is irrelevant to the American scene. Thus "dear Master" will not translate into an American idiom. It is an anomaly that I owe to an American the title of this study. But we have seen that Henry James acquires the rubric "Master" in a wholly European matrix, in that of Turgenev and Flaubert. American contemporaries, including William James, found the usage alien if not risible. Yet the didactic ran deep in Henry James. His journals read like tutorials of the self to the self, the critic instructing, encouraging, hectoring the creator to whom he assigns and prescribes exemplary tasks.

Inspired, in part, by the life of Daudet, James's "The Lesson of the Master" is published in the summer of 1888, a year prior to Bourget's *Disciple.* Paul Overt—note the allegory in the name—is a "young aspirant" who owes an "immense debt" to that "fine original source" embodied in Henry St. George, "the great misguided novelist." Whatever his subsequent decline, "the pardonable master" has produced *one* perfect work of art. This precedent fires Overt's imagination, though he cannot but be aware of that which is parasitic in the condition of the artist as compared to the man of action. He hopes for "the tremendous communion" between Master and disciple, despite the fact that St. George terms himself "a weary, wasted used-up animal." The lesson he imparts is the precise contrary to that given, famously, to Lambert Strether in James's *Ambassadors:* "Don't become in your old age what I have in mine—the depressing, the deplorable illustration of the worship of false gods!" The famed novelist has fallen prey to mundanity. "Stay at home and do things here—do subjects we can measure." Overt: "I'll do whatever you tell me."

James's voice rings through St. George's hymn to aesthetically rendered life: inexhaustibly, "the idea springs up—out of the lap of the actual—and shows you there's always something to be done." "Decent perfection" is fatality. James's "vitalism" borders on Nietzsche's. St. George's forty volumes are, at the last, papier-mâché. He has sold out. He has betrayed "the great thing." He cannot muster the conviction "the sense of having done the best—the sense which is the real life of the artist and the absence of which is his death, of having drawn from his intellectual instrument the finest music that nature had hidden in it, of having played it as it should be played." Marriage is the impediment: "Women don't have a conception of such things" (Nietzsche, again). Had the disciple contrived the Master's too many books, "you'd put a pistol ball in your brains." The authentic writer must "be able to be poor." The coda is merciless: "I wish you had left me alone," says the Master to his acolyte.

At stake is the axiom of Yeats's "The Choice": "perfection of the life or of the work." James falters at the noveletish dénouement. The title of the Master's magnum, *Shadowmere,* is facile. To Paul Overt he has become "the mocking fiend." As often in classic American fiction, the Faust theme lies to hand.

Attentive to models of introspection in St. Augustine, Montaigne, and Rousseau, *The Education of Henry Adams,* privately printed in 1906, remains a thoroughly American text. Conditioned by his labours as an historian, by his biographies of Albert Gallatin and of John Randolph, but principally by his experiences in Washington, Adams was committed to a characteristically American investment in political action. The point of education was public life. Disappointment, however, was inherent in the conflicts between intellectual scruple and the impurities of the democratic. "A Letter to Teachers" intimates the necessary failure. At Chartres, Adams had witnessed "the delight of its aspiration flung up to the sky." This was, in essence, the ideal motion of spirit and education. Politics and the opaque relations between energy and understanding, denied its fulfilment. R. P. Blackmur's essay of 1936, with its New Deal backdrop, puts it succinctly: Adams's was "a representative example of education: but education pushed to the point of failure as contrasted with ordinary education which stops at the formula of success." Thus in Henry Adams "his heart's hope was his soul's despair," where, in an Aquinian sense, the soul is the seat of the striving intellect. He had hoped that in certain eminent enactors of the historical process, the gap might be closed. But pondering Lincoln, Garibaldi, or Gladstone, Adams found them shallow. *The Education* is a classic of disenchantment.

Young Adams set out in deliberate quest of Masters. Harvard proved to be the first of many disappointments: "The entire work of four years could have been easily put into the work of any four months in afterlife." The sole exception were Louis Agassiz's lectures on palaeontology and the ice ages. These may have woken Adams's interest in temporalities. Germany beckoned: Goethe ranked with Shakespeare, Kant was a lawmaker to surpass Plato. Already, James Russell Lowell had imported from Germany the practice of the seminar. First came the shock of "sensual education" stemming from an encounter with the Cathedral of Antwerp and Rubens's "Descent from the Cross." "The taste of the town was thick, rich, ripe, like sweet wine." Kneeling at the foot of Rubens's depiction, Adams "learned only to loathe the sordid necessity of getting up again, and going about his stupid business." German higher education "seemed something very near to an indictable nuisance." The "derisive Jew laughter of Heine" rang through the hollow pretentions of the University of Berlin and its civic culture. The power of Beethoven came to Adams unbidden: "Among the marvels of education this was the most marvellous." Yet the experience could "not be called education, for he had never so much as listened to the music. He had been thinking of other things." It would take Adams a further forty years to enter the world of Wagner's *Ring*.

These are extraordinary notations, voluntarily, one suspects, confused and self-contradictory. They tell not only of Adams's familiarity with Kant's and Schiller's attempts to discriminate between the ethical and the aesthetic in man's schooling, but also of a thorough distrust of fin-de-siècle aestheticism, of suspect Platonism such as Walter Pater's. Adams in Antwerp, subverting his own epiphany, reads like a dissent from the arrival of Henry James's "ambassador" in the antique glow of Roman Chester. Is it likely that Henry Adams was unacquainted with Julius Langbehn's immensely influential identification of artistic eminence and national destiny in *Rembrandt als Erzieher* (*Rembrandt as Educator*), a tract which focuses also on the "teutonic, titanic" role of Beethoven?

Close comparison of the effects, brutal and oblique, of the Civil War in which neither fought, on James and on Adams, would be rewarding. For Adams, it was "to make a victim of the scholar and to turn him into a harsh judge of his masters." Such finding brought no joy. "Demolition of one's idols is painful, and Carlyle had been an idol. Doubt cast on his stature spread far into general darkness like shadows of a setting sun. Not merely the idols fell, but also the habit of faith. If Carlyle, too, was a fraud, what were his scholars and school?" The archangels of poetry, Hugo, Landor, came to bore Adams. What of the overarching systematizers and secular prophets? Some "narrow trait of the New England nature" inhibited his conversion to Marxism. Which left Comte's positivism and what access geology allowed Adams to Darwinian evolution. William Henry Seward, Lincoln's dour Secretary of State, was a true "teacher of Wisdom," but he receded from Adams's life and political hopes. As with Henry James, the sudden death of a sister, Louisa Catherine, thrown from a cab, marked the turning point: "The last lesson—the sum and term of education—began then." Much lay ahead, but in the uncertain light of an Indian summer. Now a professor at Harvard, affecting a mastery to which he did not feel entitled, Henry Adams, who had quixotically "sought education . . . must now sell it." "From Zeno to Descartes, hand in hand with Thomas Aquinas, Montaigne and Pascal, one stumbled as stupidly as though one were still a German student of 1860. Only with the instinct of despair could one force oneself into this old thicket of ignorance after having been repulsed at a score of entrances more promising and more popular . . . The secret of education still hid itself somewhere behind ignorance, and one fumbled over it as feebly as ever." Almost tacitly, the presiding truth seeps into the awareness of the reader of this fascinating, if sometimes clotted, memoir. The only authentic Master is death.

Henry Adams never relinquished altogether the dream of fiction. His second novel, *Esther,* struck him as signifying more than all his tomes of historical writings. Here is a link with Lionel Trilling, one of my predecessors in this pulpit.

The Middle of the Journey is undervalued. Together with Adams's *Democracy* and Robert Penn Warren's *All the King's Men,* it belongs to a small constellation of great American political fiction. Elsewhere, Trilling examines the enigmas of Masters and disciples. The informing background is twofold: Trilling's nervous Judaism comported alertness to that relation throughout the Talmudic and hasidic traditions. His passionate interest in Matthew Arnold evoked a man of letters himself immersed in pedagogic concerns and the transmission of "values." "Hebraism," moreover, had been among Arnold's abiding concerns.

In "Of This Time, Of That Place" (1943), the campus is a pastorale. As Joseph Howe prepares to face his first class of the year, he resolves that teaching will be by open discussion: "but my opinion is worth more than anyone else's here." Enter, in "heraldic formality," one Tertan, Ferdinand R. Undermining is immediate. The assigned essay would not be for Tertan "an extemporaneous subject." His "strange mouth" smiling, Tertan (held to be modelled on Allen Ginsberg in Trilling's course at Columbia University) strives to define Howe as a *Maître* in "the French sense." To be a valid teacher is to take one's place in the lineage of Kant, Hegel, and Nietzsche. Howe glimpses in his mutinous pupil "a medieval student who takes leave of Abelard." Tertan hands in a pretentious, pseudo-lyric paper of arresting originality. Howe is a poet in the thinnest vein, prepared "to rest easy" in a minor academic key. He comes upon a review which castigates his esoteric preciousness. Fatally, Tertan too has read the screed, but professes admiration for Howe's intent and contempt for the critic. "Tenderness" between Master and disciple is in the air.

The class is reading Ibsen's *Ghosts.* Tertan strikes at the very centre, but smothers his perception in fathomless verbosity: "Oh, the boy was mad, and suddenly the word, used in hyperbole, intended almost for the expression of exasperated admiration, became literal. Now that the word was used, it became simply apparent to Howe that Tertan was mad." "You seem to be involved," remarks the Dean to his appalled instructor. In turn, Tertan's scrawl to the Dean reveals to Howe "a power of love." In truth, "the pitiable Tertan sternly pitied him, and comfort came from Tertan's never-to-be-comforted mind." The medical verdict on Tertan is implacable. It results from inhuman "instruments of precision," Tertan's definition of the camera which he clutches in his hands on the outer rim of a commencement ceremony from which he is ostracized. Howe is smitten fiercely by a sense of the "thrice-woven circle of the boy's loneliness." Yet, at the same moment, Howe intuits that it is *he* who is being pitied, that the failure is his. He leaves Tertan a sadder and a wiser man.

"The Lesson and the Secret" of 1945 is a slighter vignette. Vincent Hammell, brilliant in theory but pragmatically useless, is teaching "Techniques of Creative Writing" to nine wealthy ladies who have, so far, sold nothing to any magazine. These aspirants pine for a guide and agent "who could give us the straight dope." Hammell reads to them an admittedly entrancing story. Yet in the listeners' "moment of brooding relaxation, there was something archaic and mythological, something latently dangerous. It was thus that the women of Thrace must have sat around Orpheus before they had occasion to be enraged with him." Old Mrs. Pomeroy, who had once mentioned Bourget(!), voices gratitude for the wonder that is literature. But it is Mrs. Stocker who triggers revolt by putting the only meaningful question: "does this writer sell well?"

◇◇◇

The complex "Master/disciple" is in no way restricted to the domains of religion, philosophy, or literature. It is not circumscribed by language or text. It is a fact of life between generations. It inheres in all training and transmission be it in the arts, in music, in crafts, in the sciences, in sport or military practise. Impulses towards loving fidelity, towards trust, towards seduction and betrayal are integral to the process of teaching and apprenticeship. The eros of learning, of imitation and subsequent enfranchisement is as susceptible to crises, to ruptures as is that of sex. Tensions concentrated and released in a Platonic *conversazione,* around a seminar table, are reproduced in the atelier, the conservatory, and the laboratory. Identical modes of rivalry, of jealousy, of lust for succession, identical tactics of treason, operate in the workshop or master class. Our threefold paradigm—the Master's destruction of his disciple, the disciple's betrayal or usurpation of the Master, the electric arc of shared faith and paternity— is ubiquitous.

Scholarship reveals how much of eminent art is collective. At numerous periods, notably medieval and Renaissance, Masters command a squad of assistants and apprentices. Behind the patron's figure, lesser hands fill in the landscape. The studio is a workshop with techniques of assembly and substitution anticipating those of manufacture. In this milieu, as Vasari tirelessly documents, jealousies, competition (sometimes homicidal), plagiarism are rife. Precisely the same mechanism characterizes the musical conservatory, the master class in composition or execution. In what French aptly calls an architect's *étude,* students and acolytes will, in turn, hive off to set up their own rival firms. If possible, just as did the goldsmiths of Nuremberg, the tapestry weavers of Antwerp, they will poach clients. Too often, the layman envisages scientific research as a locus of Olympian concord, an Arcadia of fairness. Teamwork in the sciences, in a patron's laboratory, can be fraught with jealousies, with fiercely competing egoism. Whose name will figure when the results are published? This *invidia* has become more acute as the economics of success become greater and the funding more precarious. Virtually in every human pursuit, the apprentice becomes the critic, the denier or rival of his Master. The dynamics are the more intricate where technique—the application of paint, the bowing of the violin, the drafting of a blueprint—are inseparable from exemplary stimulus and inspiration. Where mastery is of sensibility as well as of the hand. Music provides a paramount case.

Nadia Boulanger's development was meteoric. A student at the Paris Conservatoire from age nine onward, she soon "gave promise of magnificent things to come." A first prize in harmony followed in 1903. At thirteen, Nadia made her public debut on the organ and at the piano. Fauré was her inspired teacher and lasting touchstone. Having graduated with all awards in 1904, Nadia Boulanger, still in her teens, began teaching in her own right, generating both fear and respect among her students. She began a concert career in the spring of 1905, pioneering the use of the harpsichord in performances of Bach and turning to serious composition. Allowed only a second Grand Prix de Rome in 1908, Nadia Boulanger crystallized feminist protests against academic and professional injustice. The brilliance of her younger sister Lili, who had mastered music with "informal ease," complicated matters. Lili won the Prix de Rome in 1913, being the first woman so honoured. That same year also marked the beginnings of Nadia Boulanger's celebrity as a pedagogue. Gifted pupils streamed to her. The first child prodigy to be instructed, Jacques Dupont, was brought to her at the age of two. An informal beehive of older girls, the "Nadia Boulanger Society," buzzed around the Master. Already, legend had it that she would not be promoted to a full professorship at the Conservatoire because the exercises she set were too demanding. Lili's death in March 1918, the stature of Lili's compositions, confirmed Nadia's self-denying vocation. Henceforth she would be nothing but a supreme teacher, living through her pupils in what may have been "atonement" for the obsessive but ambivalent feelings she had nursed towards her more creative junior. The posthumous cult of Lili never slackened.

Nadia Boulanger's first American student had arrived in 1906. America's entry into war inspired a Comité Franco-Américain du Conservatoire. Walter Damrosch conducted in Paris. With the close of hostilities, American artists, writers, and musicians thronged the city. Boulanger attracted American celebration and financial aid. Headed by Alfred Cortot, the new Ecole Normale de Musique finally accorded Boulanger a tenured, prestigious base. A music school for Americans, a Franco-American conservatory under Boulanger's aegis, was established at Fontainebleau. First to enroll was the twenty-year-old Aaron Copland. By the end of 1925, Nadia Boulanger had taught more than one hundred American composers and performers. These included Stanley Avery, Roger Sessions, Virgil Thomson, Donald Harris, Walter Piston, Elliott Carter. In respect both of numbers and of quality, Boulanger's *magisterium* is unparalleled in the history of music. Its effect was decisive: "She had the feeling that American music was about to take off in the way Russian music took off in the 1840s. She gave us the confidence to do it." Her charges were introduced to those who could launch their compositions. Thus Copland was introduced to Damrosch and to Koussevitzky. New forces in ballet, Ninette de Valois, Balanchine, were drawn into the Fontainebleau orbit. By the age of thirty-five, Mlle Boulanger was an international power. Her disciples constituted a phalanx of awed but also loving fidelity.

A first visit to the United States, where sometime pupils and admirers awaited her, occurred in December 1924. Boulanger's lectures at Radcliffe in 1938 are remembered still. Coaching choral groups, Boulanger introduced her own rediscovery of Renaissance motets by Monteverdi, Schütz, Dowland, and Campion. She pioneered the return to Purcell and Rameau. Almost against her will, Boulanger escaped to America in 1940. Again, her lectures and master classes drew ardent following. Returning home, she was, after candidacies extending over twenty-three years, made full professor at the Conservatoire. A new wave of American students included Gian Carlo Menotti and Leonard Bernstein. Rebels were few. George Antheil, George Gershwin found her methods unpalatable. After extended study, Philip Glass breaks away. In Paris, Olivier Messiaen and Jeune France had replaced neoclassicism. None the less, Boulanger's lectures and Wednesday classes retained great influence. Among French composers, Jean Françaix and Igor Markevitch proclaimed their debt to the "Boulangerie," the almost mythical "bakery" of musi-

cal excellence. Contact with American music remained unbroken. Boulanger's seventieth birthday occasioned a unique
tribute: "*Vive* Teacher" headlined the *New York Times.* Her
eyesight failing, her hearing as acute as ever, Nadia Boulanger
taught choral singing incomparably to the very end. She died
at ninety in October of 1979.

Her views and sensibility were nothing less than hybrid.
Committed to the American experience, seminal in American musical history, Nadia Boulanger never reneged on the
conviction that Europe was and would continue to be Athens
whereas the United States was destined to be Rome. Surrounded by disciples of Jewish provenance, Boulanger's worship of discipline, of informing authority, led her to sympa-
thize with the fascism of the Action Française, antisemitism
included! This may, in part, account for her unwillingness to
come to terms with Arnold Schoenberg. Indeed, her ear for
contemporary music proved fitful: enthused by the *Rite of
Spring* when she was nineteen, Boulanger's responses to Stra-
vinsky turned ambivalent. Atonality disturbed a passionate
disciple of Fauré and, later on, of Lully. She delighted in the
baroque virtuosity of her student Ralph Kirkpatrick.

No one who has not been a Boulanger pupil can articulate
what must have been the spell of her teaching. The *dicta* tend
to be of monumental generality: "I don't believe in the teaching of aesthetics unless it is combined with a personal inter-
change." To her Radcliffe choristers: "Do not merely the best
you can; do *better* than you can!" "May I have the power to
exchange my best with your best." Or, in 1945: "The teacher
is but the humus in the soil. The more you teach, the more
you keep in contact with life and its positive results. All considered, I wonder sometimes if the teacher is not the real stu-

dent and the beneficiary." Ten years later: "When I teach, I throw out the seeds. I wait to see who grabs them . . . Those who do grab, those who do something with them, *they* are the ones who will survive. The rest, *pfft!*" And in the *Musical Journal* for May 1970: "One can never train a child carefully *enough* . . . we must do everything we can for the one who can do very much, and it is unfair to our human justice. But human justice is a small justice" (how Plato and Goethe would have agreed).

Anecdotes illustrating Nadia Boulanger's technical mastery abound. They tell of her ability to spot instantaneously the minutest error or oversight in a student's performance; of her anger at any mode of compositional or executant bluff; of a memory beyond compare. One suspects, however, that the genius lay elsewhere, that it would have characterized whatever discipline she taught. Boulanger's engagement in the act of teaching was absolute, "totalitarian" in the rarest sense. Her axiomatic insight that talent, that creativity are not subject to social justice underwrote not only her own elitism but that of her students. She gave them the confidence to become what they were. This is a Master's supreme donation. As Ned Rorem put it, Nadia Boulanger was quite simply "the greatest teacher since Socrates."

◇◇◇

To Pindar and Plato, the point would have been obvious. If philosophy, literature, and music have their Masters and disciples, so does sport. On the American scene the figure of the coach is iconic. From the backwater high school to the professional apex, the coach is held in fervent esteem. College and university presidents, let alone their professors, command far smaller salaries than the astronomical remunerations of football or basketball gurus. A President of the United States came to pay valedictory hommage to "Bear" Bryant, inspirer of the University of Alabama's "crimson tide." But in the hall of fame, Knute Rockne stands supreme.

His talents were manifold: as teacher of chemistry, as actor and skilled flautist. Rockne became a public speaker as immediately recognizable as was Rudolph Valentino. Of Norwegian immigrant stock, he played for Notre Dame in a famous 1913 victory over the U.S. Military Academy, a game which helped make of the forward pass a lethal weapon. Assistant football coach in 1914, Rockne was made head coach and director of athletics four years later. The thirteen seasons that followed established a peerless record: one hundred and five wins against only twelve losses and five ties. Three national championships. With their legendary "Four Horsemen" in the backfield and "Seven Mules" on the line of scrimmage, the 1922–24 Notre Dame teams were virtually invulnerable. The Magus transformed tactics, launching blitz attacks out of the T-formation, substituting fresh teams, his "shock troops," in the course of the game. Extraordinary as was his generalship on the field, Knute Rockne's true eminence lies in his generation of a lineage of coaches without parallel in any other sport (or pedagogic enterprise). He was, incomparably, a teachers' teacher, a Master whose disciples would, in turn, disseminate and perfect his doctrines.

At the time of Rockne's death, in an airplane crash in Kansas in March 1931, more than two hundred athletes who had played for him had entered the coaching profession. Ninety among them in colleges, almost forty as head coaches. To have played under Rockne meant an assured coaching job on graduation. Twelve senior coaches were alumni of the 1919 squad, eleven emerged in 1922. They inculcated Rockne's ideas and drill across the continent. Particularly in the Midwest, at Michigan, at Purdue, the Rockne model created powerhouses in football and, by osmotic glory, in academic standing. Yet the Master insisted that his methods were an open book. They amounted to choreographic detail and discipline in the execution of a clutch of basic plays, a precision which bred unbeatable confidence. Knute Rockne regarded his disciples as family. He maintained close personal touch, dispensing professional and personal advice, sending wedding presents, inquiring about wives and offspring. Reciprocally, former Notre Dame players, even when they were not coaching, acted as scouts, scrutinizing, reporting back on adversaries. Accurate readings of Stanford's style contributed to a famous win at the 1925 Rose Bowl. "Dope on Carnegie Tech" from a faithful spy allowed Rockne to avenge his first home loss in twenty-three seasons.

Beginning in 1922, Rockne Coaching Schools imparted the Notre Dame philosophy and its techniques. Summer sessions were organized in seventeen locations with Notre Dame players as instructors. As a result, thousands of high school and collegiate mentors were to adopt Rockne's general axioms and specific plays. This "coaching tree" bore illustrious fruit. From it stemmed "Bear" Bryant and Vince Lombardi (of the Green Bay Packers in Wisconsin). At Notre Dame itself, Frank Leahy proved to be an innovative heir.

This entire genealogy remains of extreme historical and methodological interest. A local, in many ways almost esoteric pastime—American football does *not* speak the world language of football, of a *Cupa Mundial*—became a national passion owing, largely, to the genius of a Master. What other *paideia* has been as prolific of excellence? Rockne's disciples trained a third generation of didactic leadership. Many of their practices survive into the changing game of the twenty-first century. Somehow, Knute Rockne was able to exemplify, to transmit a technically perfected common sense of victory. There was no Pindar to immortalize his charismatic prowess, but more than one hundred thousand mourners traveled to South Bend for the funeral. More than for Browning's grammarian.

◇◇◇

In the United States, over these past decades, two movements or pathologies have eroded trust between Master and disciple, between the teachers and the taught.

Eros and teaching are inextricable. This is true prior to Plato and after Heidegger. Modulations of spiritual and sexual desire, of domination and submission, the interplay of jealousy and faith, are of a complication, of a delicacy which defy exact analysis (in his seminar on the *Symposium,* Leo Strauss found the issue of love to be almost intractable). Components are subtler than gender, than demarcations between homo- and heterosexuality, between what are judged conventionally to be licit and prohibited relations with the young. Role reversals occur constantly: it is Beatrice, the beloved child, the adored woman, who becomes the Master-Mistress of the Pilgrim's soul. In Shakespeare's sonnets, the *pas-de-deux* of instruction and desire, of bestowal and reception touches on depths beyond paraphrase. Even consummate bodily possession is a small thing compared with the fearsome laying of hands on the quick of another human being, on its unfolding, implicit in teaching. A Master is the jealous lover of what might be.

Unquestionably, there are dangers. The eros of intellect, fiercer than any other, can shade into lust. It can trigger exploitative sadism, both mental and physical. Perceptions of this degeneration abound in Balzac, in Dickens, in the Henry James of *The Portrait of a Lady*. The emotional or professional needs and hopes of the disciple, his or her psychic and material dependence on the Master's favours can provoke, indeed invite sexual pressures. Socrates in the *Symposium,* the *Magister Ludi* in Hesse's fable, are acutely aware of the trap. It seems to have disturbed Wittgenstein. At lesser levels, such exactions make for catastrophe. If there is in Mastery, in the pedagogic, a "sin against the Holy Ghost," it is the sexual use of the pupil in exchange for commendation and advancement. The fact that this exchange can be initiated by the victim, that sexual favours are on hopeful and calculated offer in the teaching situation, only makes the bargain uglier. Submission can be the most unnerving of assaults.

To this immensely complex theme, older than Alcibiades or "the beloved disciple," "sexual harassment" in the American manner has contributed menace and trivialization, cynicism and the arts of blackmail. Intimacy of tone between teacher and student, unguarded warmth or ease of gesture, have been made culpable. Doors must be left open lest privacy be abused. Blameless lives have been pilloried or destroyed by accusations which are, by their nature and hysterical edge, nearly impossible to disprove. The nastiness is particularly rife in the humanities where young women now account for the great majority of pupils and where literature and art are inevitably charged with erotic content and suggestions. That charges of harassment *have* been justified is certain, that the crazed competition for academic chances has led to abuse is undeniable. In far too many instances, however, such accusations have been the result of mendacious hysteria, of opportunistic frivolity. The cost has been ruinous. It is witnessed in David Mamet's *Oleanna* or, in a South African setting, in J. M. Coetzee's *Disgrace.* Strains of Puritanism, of legalism, endemic in American history, have been unleashed. Irony, which is the leaven of understanding, has been rendered even more suspect than it already was throughout the American ethos.

Abstention from irony, from alertness to ridicule which should mark adult sensibility, also characterizes the witch hunts of so-called "political correctness." Again, there are valid grounds. Neglect of the history and achievements of ethnic minorities, of the tragic legacy of slavery in North America, of the manifold contributions of the black community to American destiny, was indeed scandalous. As was the failure to inquire into, to commemorate and value the role of women long made mute by male domination and patriarchal prejudice. Or consider our debilitating ignorance of Islam. An anachronistic injustice called for repair.

What has too often ensued, however, is a travesty of responsible argument and scholarship. Artificially hyped and factitious oralities, folk texts, sub- and anti-literacies have been exalted. Pseudo-curricula have been institutionalized at the price of indispensable disciplines, creating not liberation but new ghettos for the African American or the Chicano. History has been rewritten to the point of parody. The truth is that for better or worse (I have spent a working lifetime urging the question of the correlations between the humani-

ties and the inhuman), our heritage in the west is that of Jerusalem, Athens, and Rome. The alphabet of our recognitions
is that developed by "dead white males." Our literary, philosophical, aesthetic touchstones are those of a European and
North American core, often vividly influenced from outside
and now qualified and enriched by ethnic plurality. To regard
Sophocles or Dante or Shakespeare as somehow tainted by
imperialist, colonialist mentality is idiocy pure and simple.
To discard western poetry or the novel from Cervantes to
Proust as "male chauvinistic" is blindness. As is the renunciation of the creative force of grammars and developed vocabularies under pressure of linguistic vandalism and diminution.
That Bach and Beethoven actualize reaches of human endeavour surpassing rap or heavy metal, that Keats challenges
insights of which Bob Dylan's lyrics are innocent, is or ought
to be self-evident whatever the political-social connotations
—and these do exist—of such conviction.

With honourable exceptions, the treason has once more
been that of the clerics. Academics, cultural critics, historians
have howled with the wolves in hope of popularity or forgiveness. Penitential masochism flourishes. It is the teachers (and
their frightened deans) who have broken the "Hippocratic
oath" to seek out truth, to aim for clarity of judgement, to
chance unpopularity, which a teacher must risk, be it in silent inwardness, when entering on his or her calling. Consequences, so far as the trivialization of the syllabus, of the examination process, of college and university appointments, of
serious publication and funding go, have been damaging. In
the humanities today, too many listings of courses derive
their ghostliness from the remembrance of that which is no
longer taught, from the proscription of taboo questions.

Parallels have been drawn between the witch hunts at Salem and the enforcement of political correctness. Elementary statements regarding the origins and ubiquity of slavery inside Africa, recalling the exponential genius of Greek thought, observing the global resonance of certain western languages and canonic texts, have been gagged. Teachers and scholars have been hounded, spurious "revisionists" richly rewarded. The sciences know no such folly. This crucial point is frequently overlooked. The inheritance of Archimedes, Galileo, Newton, and Darwin stands secure. (Which at no point signifies the omission of, say, Indian mathematics or early Chinese technology.) In science, bluff, let alone falsification on grounds of race, gender, or ideology is, so far as is humanly possible, ruled out. The correctness is that of the equation, not of the politics of cowardice. It is this difference, one conjectures, which helps account for the comparative prestige and dignity, at present, of the sciences and of humane letters.

Among the finest of American novelists have addressed this infirmity. In Philip Roth's *The Dying Animal* (2001), the vulgarities of heart are, presumably, intentional. The elderly Master and his young student live "the chaos of sex" turbulent in poetry, inwoven with the attempt to give imagination form, as did aging, sexually tormented Yeats. No less than the act of teaching itself, the arc of sex must cross the age gap. Incisively: "I am the author of her mastery of me." The "blowjob in the library is the campus black mass," fulfilling not the student's submission or servitude but a satiric, bacchic triumph. "Sex is also the revenge on death." On this motif, Roth's caustic intelligence rings changes at once of irony and desolation. For the narrator, "didacticism is my destiny." It must subvert and enact "the hothouse passion of the teacher-student taboo." In the all-too-willing young women, the entrancing "Gutter Girls," lurk the Maenads. Who harasses whom?

Published a year earlier, Saul Bellow's *Ravelstein* is of another substance. The classically schooled, Falstaffian protagonist, with his brazen elitism in the life both of the mind and of the senses has, near the close of his prodigal existence, achieved celebrity and fortune. The portrait is held to be that of Professor Alan Bloom and his blockbuster, *The Closing of the American Mind.* Ravelstein's Platonic concerns, references to Machiavelli and Hobbes, point no less to that of the University of Chicago sage Leo Strauss. Ravelstein has his set: "Its members were students he had trained in political philosophy and longtime friends. Most of them were trained as Ravelstein himself had been trained, under Professor Davarr and used his esoteric vocabulary." Among them are eminent public servants, journalists, and members of think tanks. The telephone makes possible an ongoing seminar in which matters arising in Washington or Paris "are aligned with the Plato they studied two or three decades ago, or Locke, or Rousseau, or even Nietzsche." The Master's lesson is unsparing: "He would tell you about your soul, already thin, and shrinking fast—faster and faster."

Ravelstein sees to it that his disciples are "soon more familiar with Nicias and Alcibiades than with the milk train or the ten-cent store." The more fortunate, the more gifted would be led through Plato and Maimonides (the Strauss syllabus) and the "higher humanity of Shakespeare—up to and beyond Nietzsche." Ravelstein's acolytes come to see their Master as a kind of Michael Jordan, the basketball superstar. Ravelstein, in this radically American analogy, levitates above the world as he expounds Plato's *Gorgias* "literally in sight of the steel mills and the ash heaps and street filth of Gary." To them, this man of "blind greed for penny candies or illegal Havana cigars was himself a Homeric prodigy." His young men "are mad for him," miming his gait (as I saw young scientists seeking to mime Oppenheimer's), his arcane musical tastes, his increasingly opulent clothes.

Saul Bellow does not flinch from the crux: "he was a teacher, you see. That was his vocation—he taught. We are a people of teachers. For millennia, Jews have taught and been taught. Without teaching, Jewry was an impossibility." With his friend Herbst—the name signifies autumn—Ravelstein concludes that "it is impossible to get rid of one's origins, it is impossible not to remain a Jew. The Jews, Ravelstein and Herbst taught, following the line laid down by their teacher Davarr [was Bellow thinking of Paul Shorey?], were historically witnesses to the absence of redemption." I will return to this point.

Eros and the classics are never far apart. The more so when taught by Mr. Sypher, "Balding, cologned, mild-mannered," in Anthony Hecht's "The Mysteries of Caesar." He listens with imperturbable patience "and a somewhat cryptic smile" as his pupils misconstrue the *Gallic Wars*. Despite the "torts and tortures of grammatic laws,"

> They rather liked Mr. Sypher, who was kind,
> An easy grader. Was he a widower?
> It was thought he had lost a child some years before.
> Often they wondered what passed through his mind
>
> As he calmly attended to their halt and crude
> Efforts, not guessing one or another boy

> Served as Antinous to that inward eye
> Which is the pitiless bliss of solitude.

The reference, a "cypher" for all but the highly literate, is serenely placed. Antinous, golden boy to a stoic, lonely emperor. A schoolroom and Latin lesson haunted in a new world which is also ancient.

Anne Carson "who lives in Canada" is perhaps the most inward, enigmatic voice in contemporary poetry, her spirit possessed by the Greek epic and lyric exemplars. Greek metrics and Socrates to Phaedrus discoursing on love inform her poems. But the doomed epiphany occurs in a Latin class:

> late spring, late afternoon, the passive periphrastic,
> for some reason I turned in my seat
> and there he was.

Syntax becomes omen:

> Useless to interpose analysis
> or make contrafactual suggestions.
> *Quid enim futurum fuit si* . . . What would have
>   happened if, etc.
> The Latin master's voice
> went up and down on quiet waves. A passive
>   periphrastic
> may take the place of the imperfect or pluperfect
>   subjunctive
> in a contrary-to-fact condition.
> *Adeo parata seditio fuit*
> *ut Othonem rapturi fuerint, ni incerta noctis timuissent.*
> So advanced was the conspiracy

that they would have seized upon Otho, had they not
        feared the hazards of the night.
Why do I have
this sentence in mind
as if it happened three hours ago not thirty years!
Unshielded still, night now.
How true they were to fear its hazards.

Who says that the American and/or Canadian mind is closing?

6

UNAGING INTELLECT

◇ ◇ ◇

WE HAVE SCRATCHED the surface. There is no community, no creed, no discipline or craft without its Masters and disciples, its teachers and apprentices. Knowledge is transmission. In progress, in innovation, however trenchant, the past is present. Masters guard and enforce memory, Mother of the Muses. Disciples enhance, disseminate, or betray the personal and social sinews of identity. We have seen how interactive these dynamics are. The concept of an autistic Master, incapable of, refusing to, share his findings is logically possible but verges on contradiction. What can we know of a "mute Milton" (though we have noted refusals to communicate the *doxa* or discovery lest it fall into evil hands)?

To "cover" the field would be an absurd ambition. The languages required, the ethnographic, anthropological, historical, and scientific expertise needed, are much beyond any individual witness. The Mastery of the Shaman, of the almost liturgic storytellers of the Kalahari or the South Pacific, the initiations to apprenticeship, often esoteric and barred to any outside observer, in African, southeast Asian, Islamic cultures are accessible, if at all, to a handful of specialists. Even the most successful, global of faiths, ideologies, scientific conjectures and techniques, are only the all-too-visible tip of an iceberg of teaching whose hidden mass reaches into the depths of the human experience. Astrologers vastly outnumber professors of astrophysics. It may well be that their influence on the more fundamental, "organic" levels of consciousness is far greater.

None the less, two traditions—it might be better to say "two worlds," for such is their seniority and wealth—must be cited; though my lack of competence in the relevant languages and texts will make reference wholly inadequate.

"Without teaching," says Bellow, "Jewry was an impossibility." Judaism is uncompromisingly pedagogic. The teaching situation is inherent in Judaic monotheism. The incessant dialogue between God and the Jew has, since Abraham, exhibited every aspect of the magisterial relation with a people of adoring, mutinous, obedient, recalcitrant, but above all of a *questioning* nature. The Torah imparted to and through Moses, the Psalms inspired in David, the books of prophecy and proverbs, constitute a syllabus, a manual for daily instruction and use. The Jew is perpetually *examined,* in a sense which differs from the axiom of "examined life" in Socrates. His schooling lasts as long as he lives. Singular to this didactic relation is the range of the dialogue. It reaches from ecstatic adoration and submission to bitterest irony, to moral protest as in Job. It comprises the response of the celebrant, echoing the voice of God in the liturgy, to dissent and even indictment (as in Paul Celan's despairing "counter-Psalm"). In the most concrete sense, the survival of Judaism has hinged on this millennial exchange in the classroom or the synagogue, in the Talmudic school and the often mysteriously "binomial" tutorial within the individual, private conscience. As the Jewish joke goes: "don't speak to me while I'm interrupting you." The God of Israel is headmaster in a *shul* which is the world.

It is the constancy of this didactic discourse which preserves Jewish identity even when the national and material conditions of Jewish existence are virtually snuffed out. After the destruction of the Temple and the triumph of Roman rule, Akiba and his disciples kept Torah study and commentary ardently vital. The unbroken lineage of talmudic explicators, of teachers and exegetes springs out of, flourishes within exile and persecution. Rabbinic classes were held in the death camps. The commandment to study Torah each and every day is set, by certain rabbinic authorities, even above the commandment to love and honour God, Torah study being, precisely, the enactment of such love. Hence the unparalleled prestige of the teacher in the Jewish tradition and community. Hence also the recurrent intuition, which Wittgenstein found morosely persuasive, that the genius of the Jew is one of study and exposition rather than of original creation. What is there to add to what God has created? The Jewish homeland is the text, wherever on earth it is committed to memory, minutely perused, and made the object of unending commentary (cf. Freud's "unending analysis"). Jewish mythology *par excellence* is the teeming chronicle of the tales of the Masters and of the illustrative episodes which attend on their teaching.

The traditions of such teaching are bewilderingly diverse.

They extend from the ultra-orthodox and fundamentalist to the heretical and the antinomian. Torah and Talmud instruction is one thing; that of the Kabbalah, with its own prodigal narratives of mastery and discipleship, is quite another. Compendious as it is, written material is a fraction of the whole; orality has long been, continues to be predominant. The quest for understanding inhabits the living word, the face-to-face to which Emmanuel Levinas has given hermeneutic primacy. Nowhere are the relations between Masters and disciples mythologized, dramatized more insistently than in the tales, memoirs, sayings of the Hasidim, the movement of pietism, in some regards mystical, founded in eighteenth-century Poland by the Baal Shem Tov, Master of masters. It is in the rabbinic "courts," in the schools and shtetls of eastern Europe, of Poland and the Baltic states, that Israel's self-definition as discipleship, as apprenticeship to God, attains its most intense pitch. No brief survey can begin to do justice to the dialectical finesse, to the intellectual resource, to the irony, humour, pathos, and at times explosive joy—when the soul dances—of the surviving material. Though the world which it "bespeaks" is now ash. This material has been gathered and retold by Martin Buber, by Elie Wiesel, by scholars of ethnography and comparative religion. Its influence on secular writers such as Kafka, Borges, and Bellow makes for a fascinating chapter. Via Harold Bloom and Levinas, it has entered the idiom of modern poetic and poststructuralist philosophy. "Scholem" and "Golem" rhyme in more than one context.

Legends surrounding the Baal Shem are legion. Scholars distinguish the visionary, almost shamanistic aspects from teaching which is enmeshed in the humblest immediacies of daily existence and need. The Master dances with the scrolls of the Torah. Charisma emanates from his person, from his enigmatic clairvoyance. He is a virtuoso of parable. Asked by a disciple why we experience a sense of infinite remoteness at the very moment when we cling to God, the Baal Shem replies: "when a father teaches his little son to walk, he holds his two hands on either side, closely, lest the child fall down; but when the child is nearest to him, he holds his hands farther apart so that his son may learn to walk on his own." Though rooted in a Jewish community of exceptional fervour and unfolding, the Baal Shem harboured no illusions. Like Israel itself, "truth is driven out of one place after another, and must wander on and on." He taught as he breathed. His last words were an act of teaching, a magisterial exposition of a verse from the Book of Esther.

Three teachers' teachers came after him: the Maggid of Mezritch, Pinhas of Koretz, and, to a more fitful degree, Yehiel Mikhal of Zlotchove. It is the Maggid's hasidic school which remains the principal font of teaching legends. As Buber puts it, for the Maggid the universe can be understood only "from the viewpoint of God's educational methods." He would not tell his disciples who among them had arrived at the correct interpretation of his instruction. Whichever of the seventy facets of the Torah one ponders with a truthful spirit, with unwavering attentiveness, will yield truths. The Maggid lit the candles in his disciples' consciousness. But it is they who must scrutinize and tease out, over lengthy, concentrated periods of meditation, the cornucopia of meanings in a single saying or textual fragment. Ascetic ecstasy, which had marked the Maggid's early repute, modulated into pedagogy. Because teaching had become his living breath, the Great Maggid, as he was known, did not write a book. Like Socrates, he entrusted enlightenment to the spoken word. He allowed his words to "be taken down"—a telling idiom. Instead of a written corpus, he composed only disciples and disciples of disciples. His son, the Kabbalist mystic Rabbi Abraham, went further: he gave instruction to one disciple only, Shneuer Zalman, for to externalize via teaching in inward revelation is to "descend to the lowest rung." Even today, the very few Masters of Kabbalah will, during their lifetime, attend to only one or two apprentices.

Rabbi Pinhas is thought to have been the disciple most faithful to the spirit and example of the Baal Shem. He was known to his awed contemporaries as "the brain of the world." His relations, personal and doctrinal, to his disciple Rafael of Bershad was one of pure loyalty and accord. It endures as a golden page in the so often troubled history of Masters and disciples. Rabbi Yehiel Mikhal takes us to the threshold of the nineteenth century. This ascetic *zaddik,* or "just one," was an inspired itinerant preacher. An aura of myth accompanied his sudden presences and withdrawals, the illumination he brought, as it were, out of the night. Though his actual teachings revealed paradoxical, even antinomian readings of the holy word, he was revered, in a resplendent phrase, as "the soul of the soul." Perhaps a teacher can aspire to no prouder title.

Providentially, Menahem Mendel of Vitebsk, one of the three hundred disciples that tradition ascribes to the Maggid, transported the hasidic movement to Palestine. Followed by a troupe of students, he went there in 1777. Tradition has it that his pupil Aaron of Karlin was so eloquent as to deprive his listeners of the uncertainties and freedom of moral choice.

Wherefore God took his young life. Wandering Masters made of their peregrinations an *imitatio* of God's self-banishment from the world as it is taught in certain kabbalistic conceits. Rabbi Zalman, "the Rav," founded a particularly fruitful Lithuanian branch of hasidism. His teachings can incline towards rationalism, striving to bridge the increasingly acerbic gap between hasidism and traditional rabbinic orthodoxy. At the same time, Zalman was a renowned singer and dancer, singing as did Socrates, dancing wisdom as Nietzsche enjoins. In midst the ascetic impulses of hasidism, the Song of Songs plays an eminent role. Its joyous eroticism translates into the passion for intimacy with God. The Masters invoked a paradoxical "lust for purity."

No anthology of hasidic dicta gives a fair view of their challenging force. Time and again, the stress lies on transmission. Thus Barukh of Mezbizh: "When a word is spoken in the name of its speaker, his lips move in the grave. And the lips of him who utters the word move like those of the Master who is dead." "I did not go to the Maggid to hear Torah," recalls Rabbi Leib, "but to see how he unlaces his felt shoes and laces them up again." Pinhas of Koretz reminded his students that "the soul teaches incessantly, but never repeats itself." Wit sharpens the dialectic. In a pre-Nietzschean tone, Rabbi Zusya of Hanipol urged: "In the coming world, they will not ask me: 'Why were you not Moses?' They will ask me: 'Why were you not Zusya?'" "Become what you are." Study is salvation: when man reaches the other world, he will be asked: "who was your teacher, and what did you learn from him?" (Shelomo of Karlin). Yet even the most devoted study is as nothing: Rabbi Israel of Konitz had immersed himself in eight hundred books of the Kabbalah; when he came to the

Great Maggid, he knew instantly that he knew nothing at all. Consoling an unsuccessful colleague, Rabbi Jacob Yitzakh came close to defining the core of great teaching: "they come to me because I am astonished that they come, and they do not come to you because you are astonished that they do not come." Throughout the hasidic and rabbinic worlds, the house of study is also the house of prayer (*Beth ha-Midrash*). The traveller, homeless in body or in soul, is made welcome.

Martin Buber gathered the tales of Rabbi Nachman, the great-nephew of the Baal Shem who taught in Palestine during 1798–99. Nachman was convinced that it is by a wonder of resonance that the Master hears from the disciple the most hidden insights. With his death, so Buber, the major mystical lineage dies out: "Joy gives the spirit a homestead; sadness drives it into exile." Today, only vestiges remain. Barbarism hounded to extinction the relevant communities, their language, their memories. But in the records of Mastery and discipleship, of the wonder and strangeness of the teacher's calling, hasidism wrote a nearly unrivalled page. Nowhere have there been truer "singing masters" of the human soul.

◇◇◇

Entrancement with "the light from the East," hope for occult revelations out of Asia, for techniques of purification and of meditation allowing access to the transcendental, have been perennial throughout western culture. We know of the spell that Egyptian and Persian arcana exercised on Pythagorean and Platonic schools. "Guru" comes to us via Hindu and Sikh usage. Successive modes of European and Anglo-American interest have fashioned their own "passages to India" (compare the connotations of that phrase in Walt Whitman

and in E. M. Forster), their own images of Taoism, Buddhism, and Zen. The current fascination dates back to the
"parliament of religions" held in Chicago in 1893. Via such
acolytes as Hermann Hesse and Aldous Huxley, these constructs inspired literature, the arts, music, and psychotherapy.
They relate, especially after their diffusion in the California
of the 1950s, to the Nirvanas of narcotics, of Yoga, of commu-
nal asceticism or reverie. These characterize what may be genuine as well as the kitsch of the "New Age." A certain Pacific-
coast daydream, shot through with what are taken to be Indian, Chinese, and Far Eastern revelations, lies at the restless
heart and dread of emptiness in modernity.

This is the problem. The material is so various, so tainted
by derivative, parasitic amateurism and pretense, that the authentic source recedes out of reach. A dozen languages and
alphabets, of extreme arduousness, an acquaintance with millennia of religious, philosophic, and social history, some personal submission to codes of feeling, of bodily discipline alien
to almost all occidental practise, are a prerequisite to any reliable understanding. Even the best qualified of western orien-
talists, ethnographers, and students of comparative religion,
such as Charles Malamoud, can survey only a fraction of the
ground. Buddhism and Confucianism proliferate in Indian,
Chinese, Tibetan, Ceylonese, Burmese, and Japanese forms,
each of which divides into further ramifications esoteric and
public, hermetic and declared. Western scholars and trans-
lators have sought to interpret for us the meanings of the
Tao, of the rites fundamental to Confucianism, of the rituals
of the Veda as these unfold "Inside the Texts, Beyond the
Texts," to borrow Michael Witzel's title. A restricted number
of western men and women have had personal experience of

Asiatic monasticism, notably Shinto. Such true scholars and adepts look with more or less polite contempt on the back-packer's pilgrimage and the digests of the journalist. A fair number of the Masters of Zen regard several years of silent meditation as an indispensable, if inadequate, prelude. Ignorant of the languages, of the context of spirit and community, I can only touch, and in passing, on what are no doubt elementary and secondhand banalities. An almost closed world lies beyond.

Mastery and discipleship are the instrument of Chinese Confucianism and its complex religious, ritual background. Archetypes, familiar to us, are abundant. What deeper betrayal can there be, asks Confucius, than the death before their Master of such disciples as Tse-lou and Yen Houei, best qualified to carry on his teaching? Always open is the question of whether the Master's doctrines can be spoken, can be transmitted verbally. What, then, constitutes a perfect lesson? "The Master has barely uttered two words when the disciple falls asleep and starts snoring. The Master is enraptured: 'My disciple's body is like dead wood, his heart like cold ash. His knowledge is now truthful! He has detached himself from all acquired knowledge. Ignorant and in darkness, he has no more thoughts. One need no longer discuss with him! Ah! what a fine fellow!'" The point being the achievement of that vacancy of self and spirit which alone gives access to meditation and the core of being.

When Buddhism enters China about 65 A.D., it is already some five centuries old and replete with legendary Masters and sages. Relations with Taoism and Confucianism will be those of rivalry and reciprocal insemination. Generations will labour over translations from Sanskrit. In the patriarch

Bodhidharma, who comes to Canton in 527, the traits of the magisterial sage are fully deployed. Hauntingly, we find a motif already familiar: when the Master bids his disciples adieu and vanishes in the mountains, only a sandal is found. Shades of Empedocles. Though canonic scriptures are the object of constant veneration and commentary, it is oral transmission of insights beyond words and concepts, much of it destined to the esoteric and the secret, that remains crucial.

The practices of Zen, a transliteration of Chinese *tch'an,* reach Japan at an early date, but become prominent only after 1200. They fell on ready ground. The very word *samurai* signifies "follower." Obedience, harsh physical training, were native to Japanese mores. Kendo, "the way of the sword," and other martial arts correspond intimately to the drill of Zen. Archery, where the archer, emptied of himself, seeks the blank centre of his target, allegorizes the obedient soul. Calligraphy, garden design are approaches to a totality whose unfathomable depth resides in the minutest detail (as in the mystique of the letter in Kabbalah). The minimalism of the haiku is implosive, radiating through concentration. Eternity is experienced in an instant, in "a grain of sand." These usages make of Zen the conduct of life of an elite whose commerce with imperial power and commonplace existence will never be unambiguous.

It is in 1227 that the revered Dogen Zenji composes a mantra chanted to this day:

> Honoured disciples, follow on the legitimate lineage
> Of the patriarchs, if you persevere you shall be
> As they are. Your treasure chamber will open of itself,
> And you will draw on it to your heart's desire.

Koun Ejo refines the tactics of "self-annihilation": "even if eighty-four thousand illusory thoughts arise and vanish in you, so long as you allow them no importance and let them be, there may spring from each of them the marvellous wonder of the light of the great wisdom." Such "empty luminosity, which blazes spontaneously, is located far beyond mental energy." Keizan Jokin, who dies in 1325, initiates a line of direct succession of abbots lasting to this day. "To learn and to think is to remain at the door. To assume the posture of the lotus is to come home and sit in peace." Didactic and heuristic parables initiate the disciple, no less than in the method of Jesus: "A child sleeps beside his parents. It dreams of being thrashed or of falling gravely ill. Whatever the child's anguish, its parents cannot come to the rescue, for none can enter another's dreams. But if the child wakes up on its own, it will be delivered at once from its suffering." "Awakening" is the key word in Zen. Another spellbinding figure is that of the ribald, antinomian Ikkyu Sojun, reputed to have had more than one hundred ardent disciples even in old age. "Under way with my sandals and my staff, I seek out the blind donkeys who may be in quest of the truth." Frequently, the disciple must undergo humiliation and rejection before the Master's acceptance. He must pursue his chosen teacher into remote hermitages and high places; he is made to wait, perhaps for years, before the Master acknowledges his presence. Yet tradition has it that in 1740 Hakuin Ekaku instructs some four hundred disciples in the teachings of his predecessors. Both terrifying and compassionate, leonine and gentle, Ekaku dispensed "personal help and counsel as he would tea." His oral and written instruction were spread far and wide. At his death, he left ninety-one immediate disciples, founding a dynasty of abbots still in existence. The *koan* of "what sound is made when one hand is clapping?"—which has been trivialized to a cliché by western adepts—stems from Ekaku. It counts among the most elementary of the five stages of meditative questioning. It is only after his ascent into deepening abstraction and "nothingness" that the disciple is consigned to several years of solitude in final preparation for his own acts of teaching.

These narratives of abstention, of rivalry between schools and covens, of "miraculous" feats of clairvoyance and asceticism; this legacy of riddling, enigmatic, oracular pronouncements by Masters who often refuse any explanation to their disciples' anxious, reverent queries; the hagiography which surrounds the Master's wanderings, withdrawal from the world, and sanctified death—these do more than parallel Talmudic, Kabbalistic, and hasidic material. The congruities are near to uncanny. They suggest a shared typology. But the differences are, to be sure, vast. Judaism aches for direct contact and dialogue with the divine, for plenitude of revealed experience. Buddhism, particularly in its Zen version, labours towards perfect emptiness, towards the extinction of the ego in an "infinite zero" inaccessible to reason and reasoned argument. Even when surrounded by disciples, the Zen Master remains or intends to be a hermit. The phenomenon is rare in Judaism. Where it surfaces, it is in "heretic" or lapsed presences such as Spinoza and Wittgenstein.

Judaism nurtures chess masters. A Japanese elite plays Go. It may be that an outsider comes closest to some intimation of the Japanese cult of Masters and disciples via Kawabata Yasunari's reportage novel *The Master of Go,* first issued in book form in 1954. The background is factual: the defeat of Grand Master, the Honourable Inbo Shusai, by the younger Kitani Minory in a tournament played between 26th June and 4th December 1938. The Grand Master had been previously unvanquished. Ill, knowing himself to be dying, Shusai preserves a more than human serenity and self-control in the face of the vertiginous demands of the game and the skill of his adversary. At stake are the deepest meanings and paradoxes we have been looking at. "Otake," Kawabata's fictional name for the challenger, reveres his Master. To defeat him is little less than parricide. Yet to succumb would be a subtler betrayal, denying the Master's example and heritage. The bind is inescapable. Is it honourable to pursue the game against an ailing opponent who fans himself in order to waken the dying embers in the recesses of his infirm being? Two worlds now face each other. The aesthetic liberalities, the merriment of the old style of Go confront the legalistic rigorism of the new. To compromise, to overlook certain obsolete licenses and imprecisions would, in fact, do the Master dishonour. He must be defeated in strictest form. As a fearful slowness insinuates itself in Shusai's moves, Otake's own game grows dark and ponderous: "Inexorable harassment." This, in turn, offends the Master's ideal of a perfect, shared beauty. The close of the encounter offers so tortured a spectacle as to be scarcely endurable. It is the disciple who comes to the edge of breakdown. The Master stays serene in defeat. He dies shortly after the end of the match, as the snows come.

Had we but the Judaic material, and the traditions of Indian and Sino-Japanese teaching, our subject would be inexhaustible.

◇◇◇

Citing Max Brod's fiction of Tycho Brahe and Kepler, I have touched on science. In antiquity, in medieval faculties, no essential discrimination is called for: analogous relations between Masters and disciples, between *Magister* or Magus and apprentice, obtain in both humanities and sciences. Rivalries between competing philosophic and cosmological or "alchemical" schools follow a common pattern. In the Academy after Plato and Aristotle, in medical schools after Galen, in the laboratory of the alchemist and the watchtower of the astrologer, the dynamics of fidelity or insurgence, of succession or exclusion are fundamentally the same. The Faustus-Wagner relationship reflects this conjunction of theological, philosophic, and scientific conventions (science is "natural philosophy" as it had been to Lucretius). It is only with the attainment by the sciences of autonomous status, mainly during the seventeenth century, that significant differences develop. But when we try to define them, the argument is not clear-cut.

"Technique" pertains to the arts, to music, to grammar or philosophic logic no less than to the exact and applied sciences. It must be transmitted by theory and example. Yet there is a difference. The "technological," in its widest sense, is not open to spontaneous dissent and rebuttal as, again in its widest sense, is a philosophic or moral proposal. There is a determinant unison to the imparting of observational and experimental skills, a progression in difficulty characterized, more often than not, by an attendant familiarity with mathematical instruments of deepening sophistication. Individual talent matters. The demonstrator at the laboratory bench, the professor examining, will recognize exceptional quality and the potential heir. Prodigies in mathematics and the sciences are far more frequent and identifiable than in, say, poetics or metaphysics (hence what are intuited to be subterranean links between mathematics, music, and chess). Jealousies, heartbreak in the laboratory or observatory are as bitter as in the atelier and seminar. But again there is a difference, though difficult to phrase. Whatever the intrusion of psychological factors, of "elective affinities"—a concept that derives from chemistry—the emergence of the "star" has its objective, demonstrable measure. The play of feeling, of the irrational is more manifest in mastery and discipleship throughout the humanities. The agency of eros, as we have come to understand it, is far more likely. Though here also, science has its examples.

No human enterprise is *totally* value-free. A grain of ideology, of social-historical conditioning, may lodge in even the purest of abstractions. Only lunatic despotism, however, will ascribe "Jewish corruption" to the theory of relativity or seek to eradicate Mendelian genetics in the name of Stalinism. So far as is humanly possible, the mathematical theorem, the process of conjecture and refutations in science, seek out "truths"—a concept, a word of the most vulnerable fragility—independent of ethnic, religious, or political concerns. There are neither capitalist nor socialist solutions to nonlinear equations. The submission of biogenetic discoveries to financial gain is an obscenity, as is the censorship of mathematic and physical research on behalf of military purposes. Where it comes close to an ideal of disinterested, shared progress, scientific discovery is the most mature construct of human freedom.

This also differentiates the process of teaching and apprenticeship in the sciences from that in the humanities. There can be personal subversion by the disciple, by his refutation of the Master, by his adoption of a Darwinian as against a

Lamarckian model of evolution. But these will arise from necessities inherent in science itself. The Master's authentic, if often unacknowledged, triumph is to be refuted, superseded by his disciple's discovery. It is to discern in his pupil a force and futurity exceeding his own. Isaac Barrow resigns his Lucasian professorship in favour of Isaac Newton. David Hilbert does not actually question Kurt Gödel at the latter's celebratory *viva.* These men are servants to a commitment far greater than themselves.

This neutrality of truth relates to the anonymity, to the impersonality of the pure and applied sciences. Individual genius is as conspicuous in the history of the sciences as it is in that of literature and the arts. But it matters far less. The *Commedia* would not have been without Dante, the Goldberg variations without Bach. Schubert's very early death leaves spaces of sensibility unfilled. This is not so of mathematics and the sciences. It is said that an algebraic paper can reveal a personal style. Another algebraist, however, would have resolved Fermat's theorem or arrived at the Riemann conjecture. Darwin was only the most thorough, consequent of a pride of zoological and geological investigators simultaneously on the threshhold of a theory of evolution and natural selection. A dozen research centres and "atom smashers" are today at work on the same riddles in particle physics and cosmology. Publications in scientific journals, announcements on the scientific internet often carry up to thirty or more signatures. Theories, discoveries, mathematical solutions are, in a fundamental sense, both anonymous and collective, whatever the glory which accident or public relations bestows on this or that individual. Such teamwork and inevitability—the result will be achieved tomorrow if not today—

is very different from those experienced by the philosopher's disciple, by the incipient composer in a master class. There was nothing inevitable about Plato's theory of Ideas or the Sistine Chapel.

The material is diffuse. It is to be found in the biographies of eminent scientists and in their autobiographies or memoirs, which are not thick on the ground. The impersonality, the ideal anonymity of scientific research inclines to discretion. There is, moreover, a barrier to intelligible communication. Not many scientists, let alone mathematicians, have been able to narrate their labours to the layman. Technicality and the idiom of technicality, so largely mathematical, interpose. They render literary translations of the business of science artificial and, too often, erroneous. Metaphors are an awkward substitute for equations. There are novelists, Thomas Mann and Robert Musil among them, who have reimagined for us this or that corner of scientific theory and finding. C. P. Snow's early *The Search* remains valuable. On occasion, science fiction comes closest. It is this rarity that makes Richard Feynman's jazzy, corruscating self-portrayal in *Surely You're Joking, Mr. Feynman* (1985) something of what physics and astrophysics call a "singularity."

A fantastically gifted theoretician and calculator, Feynman, like Benjamin Franklin or Thomas Edison, possessed a genius for the practical, for the insights into mechanism—"how does this work, could it be made to work better?"—from which fundamental theoretical understanding may emerge. Barely out of his teens, Feynman found himself addressing the Masters. John Wheeler, Henry Norris Russell, John Von Neumann, Wolfgang Pauli, gathered to hear Feynman. Einstein joined. "These *monster minds* in front of me, waiting!"

But then, the miracle occurs: "the moment I start to think about the physics, and have to concentrate on what I'm explaining, nothing else occupies my mind—I'm completely immune to being nervous. So after I started to, I just didn't know who was in the room. I was only explaining this idea, that's all." Princeton and Los Alamos brought close meetings with giants. But it was his own collaboration with them, rather than formal teaching, that inspired Feynman. Experiments taught *him.* Even when walking with Von Neumann in the canyons, or serving as sounding board to Niels Bohr, Feynman could pursue his own irreverent originality, never accepting *prima facie* what the great man said. In turn, he became a famed teacher: "I don't believe I can really do without teaching." But the motives are psychological: the compulsion to make "*some* contribution" when blocked in his own research. Learning to draw, Feynman concluded that in physics "we have so many techniques—so many mathematical methods—that we never stop telling the students how to do things. On the other hand, the drawing teacher is afraid to tell you anything . . . The teacher doesn't want to push you in some particular direction. So the drawing teacher has this problem of communicating how to draw by osmosis and not by instruction, while the physics teacher has the problem of always teaching techniques, rather than the spirit, of how to go about solving physical problems." St. Augustine would have sympathized.

An even rarer species is that of the mathematician capable of affording the layman a whiff of his or her mysteries. Laurent Schwartz's superb autobiography, *Un Mathématicien aux prises avec le siècle* (1997), with its commitment to social justice and political action, does presume a fair degree of algebraic numeracy. Stanislaw Ulam's *Adventures of a Mathematician* (1976) is more accessible. Ulam is turbulently joyful in his recollections of apprenticeship in prewar Poland. At the time, few other nations could match the distinction of Polish mathematicians and formal logicians, the demarcation between these two fields being fruitfully blurred. What emerges from Ulam's narrative is the creative intimacy between teacher and pupil once the pupil has shown real promise. Already as a university freshman, Ulam worked closely with a group of innovative mathematicians such as Kazimir Kuratowski and Stanislaw Mazur. Osmosis, to use Feynman's term, proved crucial. Between classes, Ulam perched in the instructors' offices absorbing, virtually subliminally, their abstruse skills. The decisive gift which a Master makes to a disciple is that of a conjecture, of a problem, of a theorem as yet unproved. (Dark rumours have it that certain Masters, whether by inadvertence or malice, have directed their disciples towards trivial or insoluble tasks.) Often, the search becomes collaborative; at other times, the student is left to wrestle alone. Still a first-year tyro, Ulam solved a problem in set theory and the transformation of sets. His paper was published. As is traditional in central and eastern Europe, the café was indispensable. One session, lasting seventeen hours, involved Ulam, Mazur, and the eminent algebraic topologist Stefan Banach. (It must be haunting for a man or woman to know that a "space" has been named after them—"Banach spaces.") The murder of so many Masters by the Nazis, the systematic ravage of Polish intellectual life, injects a mournful note into Ulam's memoir.

Both Schwartz and Ulam, who was to play a vital part in the manufacture of the atom bomb at Los Alamos, are aware of the paradox whereby the "purest" of mathematical hypotheses and solutions can alter empirical and political destiny. Particle physics and information theory, which have transformed our world, are empowered by mathematical tools once regarded as recondite, speculative play. Consider the pivotal function of tensorial calculus, dormant, unnoticed, in Einstein's theory of relativity and in the equivalence of mass and energy that led to nuclear arms. Yet such is the cerebral concentration, the abstention from mundanity demanded of mathematicians—Ulam recalls spending six hours at an absolute stretch on an unsolved question in the foundations of set theory—that political, social literacy may have to come second. Hence the exceptional stature of Masters such as Schwartz or Andrei Sakharov who strove to equip their disciples with a wider perception of humane obligations.

Aristotle made fundamental contributions to logic, epistemology, and political science. So did Karl Popper. Has there been a third?

Popper's Tuesday afternoon seminars at the London School of Economics were legend. Participants and auditors have left a trove of anecdotes. Hurt to the pitch of hysteria, self-promoting, Joseph Agassi's *A Philosopher's Apprentice: In Karl Popper's Workshop* (1993) is, none the less, invaluable. The two men were in close contact from 1953 to 1960. In the Jewish manner, the disciple had chosen and sought out his Master whom he refers to as "the philosopher" (a characteristic touch): "The few years I spent in close contact with the philosopher were the most seminal in my whole life. Under his tutelage I concluded my years as a student—which began with failure and misery and, with his help and guidance, ended with excitement and progress: I learned from him how to write and how not to, how to argue and how not to, what signifies and what not, and how to do one's job as best one can. It was my period of apprenticeship with the philosopher, no doubt, that was intellectually the most exciting time of my life." Yet virtually from the start, Agassi came up against a painful interdict. Sir Karl "simply could not discuss ethics with me: even while solemnly expressing readiness to do so he sabotaged discussion on ethics. So I had a simple choice: leave or stay and quarrel and remind him repeatedly that I was an apprentice no longer." This choice was, naturally, anything but simple. Neither geographical distance—seeking academic appointment, Agassi travelled the world—nor interruptions of philosophic and personal exchanges, assuaged the disciple's torment, his thirst for the Master's acceptance and trust. Professor Agassi laboured to discriminate: "I did not want our friendship severed; I wanted my apprenticeship severed. I got the reverse of this." The disciple fights for air: "I was apprenticed to the philosopher who was thus my master—in the very old-fashioned sense of the word. As my master he educated me; as his apprentice I worked for him. It was a fair exchange, and I was very satisfied with things as they were: I did not ask for more . . . I was in charge of my fate in that I was there by choice . . . But I never promised to be a sequel to my master; I never planned to enter his shoes on his retirement. I know, in the old days the apprentice was expected to do so and marry the master's daughter too."

To complicate matters, there was savage infighting among the disciples (Agassi's chronicle has, in turn, been queried and rejected by fellow acolytes). The stellar Imre Lakatos, an epistemologist and logician of exceptional prowess, acted, according to the maddened Agassi, as if his model "was not

Iago but Stalin"—an envenomed comparison in view of ambiguities in Lakatos's Hungarian past. The seminar would seem to have seethed with competitive intrigue and back-stabbing among younger aspirants. In fact, it is doubtful whether Popper regarded as his peers anyone except such listeners as Peter Medawar and Ernst Gombrich. His set-to with Wittgenstein has become allegory. Almost invariably, members of the seminar were sounding boards for the Master's monologues. Yet the demands made were ferocious.

"The philosopher used to work day and night for at least 360 days a year." Popper reckoned that he had rewritten *The Open Society and Its Enemies* thirty times, keeping five complete versions. He worked seven days a week from dawn to midnight. When too "ill for regular work," he hammered at problems in logic. He looked to Joseph Agassi as his biographer-elect (this claim has been contested). But when Popper "began to succeed in manipulating me, I decided to change our relation drastically." The philosopher voiced his resentment to mutual friends. Bitterness and a "thankless departure" brought the relationship to an end. It is a motif we are familiar with. "Ostracized by the Master himself," Agassi deems himself better qualified to understand Popper's teachings and personality than are disciples paralyzed by fear of the Master's rejection.

Karl Popper's exigent egotism sprang from a justified sense of neglect. The epochal *Logik der Forschung* had appeared in 1935; it only achieved a measure of recognition in its English-language publication in 1959. Popper raged at extensive but unacknowledged borrowings from his works by lesser but acclaimed contemporaries. He took the most socially and academically applauded of British thinkers, of foreign origin such as his own, to be, largely, a modish sham. Honours and acceptance came very late. Correspondingly, "the philosopher" lacked grace both of heart and of intellect. His "admissions of changes of opinion are sparse and forced, as if they were admissions of some guilt. And this despite his view that change under the force of criticism is progress and that surreptitious change is among the worst intellectual crimes." To be a Jewish philosopher and political clairvoyant in the twentieth century, to be a refugee long patronized by his (very few) peers was a damaging fate. Agassi knows that his is "a gloomy record." He cannot surmount his pain at the Master's "explosive rudeness," at the "kangaroo court" and accusations of treason to which he was subjected before the final break in 1964. He protests, though aware that it will be useless "that my aim is not to be vindictive," that he wishes Sir Karl no harm.

After tragedy, the satyr play. Threats of bodily harm figure in rival accounts of the Popper–Wittgenstein encounter. Eugène Ionesco's *La Leçon* (1951) climaxes in murder. This macabre farce counterpoints Plato's *Meno,* with which we began. Its brilliance lies in Ionesco's pacing, in the masturbatory and ejaculatory rhythms which fuel the language. The dark slapstick points to the weave of eros and of sadism, of sexual humiliation and release inseparable, perhaps, from the underground of the teaching process. Power relations, always central to Ionesco, enforcement, are enacted to the point of lunacy. The Professor's sadism veers into masochism under the ferule of the Maid (shades of Strindberg and Jarry). The hypnotic turns to the homicidal comes via that most perilous of disciplines, philology. "Philology leads to the worst." Grammar and its irrational complexities incarnate authority. The student, the subliterate, the proletarian are bereft of this dominant instrument. Translation won't do:

> pour apprendre à prononcer, il faut des années et des années. Grâce à la science, nous pouvons y arriver en quelques minutes. Pour faire donc sortir les mots, les sons et tout ce que vous voudrez, sachez qu'il faut chasser impitoyablement l'air des poumons, ensuite le faire délicatement passer, en les effleurant sur les cordes vocales qui, soudain, comme des harpes ou des feuillages sous le vent, frémissent, s'agitent, vibrent, vibrent, vibrent ou grasseyent, ou chuintent ou se froissent, ou sifflent, sifflent, mettant tout en mouvement: luette, langue, palais, dents . . .

"Teeth": thirty-four piteous times, the young woman pupil mentions her worsening toothache. In vain. Monsieur will instruct, will discipline Mademoiselle whether she will or not. Interrogation verges on torture as in the White and Red Queens' questioning of Alice in Wonderland. A serial accelerando attains fever pitch:

> Je vous appelais pour aller me chercher les couteaux espagnol, néo-espagnol, portugais, français, oriental, roumain, sardanapali, latin et espagnol . . . Il suffira que vous prononciez le mot "couteau" dans toutes les langages, en regardant l'objet, de très près, fixement, et vous imaginant qu'il est de la langue que vous dites.

The corpse is removed; the doorbell rings. The Maid:

> Vous êtes la nouvelle élève? Vous êtes venue pour la leçon? Le Professeur vous attend. Je vais lui annoncer votre arrivée. Il descend tout de suite! Entrez donc, entrez, mademoiselle!

Might this fatality, this automatism of circularity be a parody of Nietzsche's doctrine of "eternal return"?

◇◇◇

In Popper's epistemology, fruitful error and falsifiability are essential. In what ways, to what ends, is it possible or practicable to teach falsehood, to impart deception? The *deceptor,* the malign demon capable of thwarting rational thought, of falsifying evidence, shadows Descartes's meditations. In the final analysis only God's love can guarantee a "teachable" because truthful reality. Descartes's wager on the reliability of the divine *magisterium* is a leap into the light. It cannot be proved. In this question of Masters of falsehood, of disciples deliberately misguided, discriminations must be drawn, but nuances and gray zones abound.

The Master can profess that "which is not," where Swift's rubric already begs every Parmenidean and Aristotelian question as to propositions that allege nonbeing, that would articulate nonexistence. Lies may be taught *knowingly*—observe the paradox. In order to persuade, to seduce on behalf of political evil, of cynical playfulness; falsehood can be taught to incite rebellion against God and His world order. This is the vast domain of the Satanic, of Milton's fallen archangel, of Simon Magus and Mephistopheles. In a secular vein, as we saw, the Sophists were charged with subverting the claims of language to ontological solidity, to authentic correspondence with substantive, verifiable being. Yet Hegel flatly states that these same Sophists were the begetters of Greek culture and of the arts of pedagogy (was not Socrates a Sophist?). Propaganda teaches lies; ideologies deliberately contaminate political, social, racial, economic material. Islam teaches its martyrs that seventy-two virgins await them in the hereafter. But how few examples are clear-cut and how difficult is refutation. Even in the exact sciences, critics such as Lakatos and Feyerabend have queried Popper's criteria of the *experimentum crucis* and of verifiability.

The imparting of falsehood can be involuntary, contingent, temporal. Shadings are manifold. News, the amended text, have not yet reached the Master. Censorship prohibits their dissemination. Errata, over centuries, can be innocent. Men of the highest integrity taught and persisted in teaching Ptolemaic cosmography or the phlogiston theory of combustion. What, on the other hand, do we say of those fundamentalists who, today, inculcate children with a flat-earth representation of the globe or who libel the theory of evolution? Yet we must be careful. Will current orthodoxies in cosmology, in physics or biogenetics prove durable? Though infrequently, even mathematics demands revision: certain Euclidean axioms are, in a larger sense, refuted by non-Euclidean geometries. We do not attach to these multiple forms and histories of error the stigma of the perverse, of culpable intent. Contingent beliefs are mutable. All teaching is provisional. It must keep open solicitations to corrective dissent. For the Sophist, such dissent is no more and no less valid than the propositions which it challenges. For the rationalist, for the liberal meliorist, it is the potential step towards a more inclusive and fertile supposition. The whole theme of "false Masters" remains to be explored. Only two are cited in Scripture, the one in Samaria (Acts 8:9–24), the other in Cyprus (Acts 13:6–12).

What I take to be incontrovertible is the belief that a Master who *deliberately* teaches untruth or inhumanity (they are the same) to his disciple comes under the category of the unforgivable. It is not, however, on this murky note that I want to conclude.

In Munich, during the winter of 1918–19, Max Weber delivered a lecture on "Science as a Vocation" (*Wissenschaft* in his title, signifying "study" and "knowledge" in the most inclusive sense) which, though imperfectly recorded, quickly became a classic. Europe lay gutted. Its high civilization, its pursuit of intellectual excellence, of which German universities had been confident safeguards, had proved powerless to arrest disaster. Would it be possible to restore to prestige and integrity that calling of the scholar, of the teacher? Weber foresaw the Americanization, the turn to managerial bureaucracy of higher learning and academic life in Europe. The gulf between "the head of such a large capitalistic academic enterprise and the old-style full professor" was yawning. In danger was the unison, which Weber judged indispensable, of scholarly-scientific research and of teaching. Criteria for promotion, now coming into force, are suspect: "The fact that students flock to a teacher is, however, determined in unbelievably large measure by purely superficial factors such as temperament and tone of voice. After quite extensive experience and sober consideration, I am very suspicious of large audiences, however unavoidable they may be. Democracy should be practised where it is appropriate. Scientific training, however, if we are to carry on with the traditions of the German universities, implies the existence of a certain type of intellectual aristocracy."

The threat to these traditions is, furthermore, internal to *Wissenschaft* itself. Our culture has embarked on a process of specialization from which it will never emerge. The outsider, the polymath is hopelessly vulnerable. In one sense, this narrowing of focus is admirable: "Whoever lacks the ability to put blinders on himself, so to speak, and to convince himself that the fate of his soul depends on whether his particular interpretation of a certain passage in a manuscript is correct, will always be alien to science and scholarship." Those incapable of experiencing "this rare intoxication" should go elsewhere. Yet such specialization may sterilize. Major hypotheses and insights can stem from "the dilettante," from the generalist or amateur (e.g. the decipherment of Linear B). Inspiration will not be programmed. The cardinal intuition "comes only when it pleases and it does not consult our desires." Be it in the humanities or in the sciences, in entrepreneurial action or the arts, creative achievement originates in what Plato called "mania." The difference is that the man of science must resign himself to the transience of his findings, that he is the servant of a progress that will cancel out or amend his labours. Only art is "fulfilment" in that no subsequent product renders it obsolete. Scientists, scholars are committed to a sacrificial ideal.

Martin Heidegger's *Rektoratsrede* was, intentionally or not, a riposte to the stoic nobility of Max Weber. Its phrasing is, as we noted, so convoluted and even esoteric as to make interpretation both hazardous and interminable. Unmistakable, however, is the identification of study and teaching, of the university *in toto,* with the destiny of the *Volk* and the demands of the national socialist revolution. Disinterested spirituality, in Kant and Weber's conception, has become an irrelevant luxury. In the new Sparta, masters are only masters under one Master. Disciples march to his drums. Even poetics reverts to its etymological roots in physical action.

Both these texts have their grandeur. But there is in Heidegger's exaltation of obedience, of discipleship more than a streak of barbarism. In its imminent wake, Yeats's image of "Sages standing in God's holy fire" (their books having been burned) took on an unbearable actuality. Nor has it lost its menace.

AFTERWORD

✧ ✧ ✧

Will the orders of relationship between Masters and disciples, as I have sketched them, persist?

A need to transmit knowledge and skills, a desire to acquire them, are constants of the human condition. Mastery and apprenticeship, instruction and its acquisition must continue so long as societies exist. Life as we know it could not carry on without them. But there are significant changes now under way.

The exponential role and authority of the sciences and of technology in the affairs of the planet go far deeper than economics or the pragmatic. They constitute a tectonic movement, a shift of gravity as far-reaching as is the gradual erosion from adult mentality of religious world views, an erosion precisely correlative with the sovereignty of the scientific. I have referred to evidence that energies and excellence of intellect are already being invested in the sciences beyond any other enterprise. This new equilibrium will be generalized.

Computation, information theory and retrieval, the ubiquity of the internet and the global web enact far more than a technological revolution. They entail transformations of awareness, of habits of perception and articulation, of reciprocal sensibility which we are scarcely beginning to gauge. At manifold terminals and synapses they will connect with our (possibly analogous) nervous system and cerebral structures. Software will become, as it were, internalized and consciousness may have to grow a second skin.

The impact on the learning process is already momentous. At his console, the schoolchild branches into new worlds. As does the student with his laptop and the researcher surfing the web. Conditions of collaborative exchange and debate, of memory storage, of immediate transmission and graphic representation have already reorganized numerous aspects of *Wissenschaft*. The screen can teach, examine, demonstrate, interact with a precision, a clarity, and a patience exceeding that of a human instructor. Its resources can be disseminated and enlisted at will. It knows neither prejudice nor fatigue. In turn, the apprentice can question, object, answer back in a dialectic whose pedagogic value may come to surpass that of spoken discourse.

As if in reaction, recourse to the therapeutic sage, to the guru and more or less secularized shaman is widespread, particularly in the insomniac west. Never have there been more faith healers, purveyors of the occult, spiritual *consiglieri*—the mafioso designation is appropriate—or cunning quacks. I have alluded to the often factitious but undeniable wave of "Orientalism" and mysticism. Even more influential are the reticulations of the psychoanalytic, the rivalries between its Masters, the covens of dependence and discipleship, which colour so many facets of our idiom and mores. Here, although in a guise which can come near to travesty, the classic motifs of mastery and discipleship flourish. In certain ways, the New Age, the climate after Freud, are pre-Socratic. Pythagoras and Empedocles would feel at home.

The charismatic aura of the inspired teacher, the romance of the persona in the pedagogic act will surely endure. At a serious level, however, the domains to which these will apply look to be increasingly restricted. More and more, the transmission of knowledge and of *technē* will rely on other means and modes of engagement. Human fidelity and betrayal, Zarathustra's commandments of love and rebellion, the one exigent of the other, are foreign to the electronic.

Women Masters have been few, though eminent. From Syracuse, Athens, Antioch onward, women disciples have been abundant. This "demography" is now altering. In the study of literature and modern languages, young women already outnumber young men. Feminization is broadening throughout the humanities and liberal arts. Women are fighting for their just place in the sun of science and technology. The patriarchal structure inherent in the relations of Master to disciple is receding. Gender identity and sexual demarcation are blurring. Nevertheless, the constructs of fidelity and betrayal, of *auctoritas* and rebellion, of mimesis and rivalry we have looked at are bound to change. In regard to her male followers—even the term "disciple" may take on a different resonance—the woman Master will develop reflexes, expectations, and symbolic motions of a novel and complex kind. Reciprocally, the male apprentice will arrive at attitudes at once devoted and, in some sense, neutral. Women disciples to women may find themselves in a situation both simplified and unstable, even if we disregard altogether the complicating pulse of the erotic. As yet, the literature is sparse and marginal. I have cited what testimony there is around Nadia Boulanger and Simone Weil. There are premonitions in the fictions of Iris Murdoch. Material is certain to increase. As yet, one can only conjecture as to unprecedented values and tensions.

The third mutation is the most important. It is also the most difficult to define. Whatever its ethnic context, whatever the relevant civilization, Mastery and discipleship have been deeply grounded in religious experience and cult. At their source, the lessons of the Masters were those of the priest. Modulation into pre-Socratic and classical philosophy was almost imperceptible. The *magisterium* of the medieval and Renaissance Master was formally that of the doctor of divinity, of Thomas Aquinas or St. Bonaventura in the chair. The theological inheritance weakened but its conventions remained in force throughout secular modernity. These forms, these conventions of spirit were underwritten by an almost unexamined, self-evident reverence. To revere one's *Maître* was the native and natural code of relationship. Where "reverence" and deference pale, a closely derived respect, a voluntary submission remains. In an enfolding sense, whose definition in the west dates back to Aristotle and Cicero, the dynamism is that of admiration, of admiring pride in the Master's stature and in his acceptance of one's discipleship. "This is our master, famous calm and dead, / Borne on our shoulders."

I would entitle our present age as that of irreverence. The causes of this fundamental transformation are those of political revolution, of social upheaval (Ortega's notorious "revolt of the masses"), of the scepticism obligatory in the sciences. Admiration, let alone reverence, have grown outmoded. We are addicts of envy, of denigration, of downward levelling. Our idols must exhibit clay heads. Where incense rises, it does so towards athletes, pop stars, the money-mad, or the kings of crime. Celebrity, as it saturates our media existence, is the contrary to *fama.* The wearing, millionfold, of the football god's jersey number or of the crooner's hairdo is the contrary to discipleship. Correspondingly, the notion of the sage verges on the risible. Consciousness is populist and egalitarian, or pretends to be. Any manifest turning towards an elite, towards that aristocracy of the intellect self-evident to Max Weber, is close to being proscribed by the democratization of a mass-consumption system (this democratization comporting, unquestionably, liberations, honesties, hopes of the first order). The exercise of reverence is reverting to its far origins in the religious and ritual sphere. Throughout mundane, secular relations the prevailing note, often bracingly American, is that of challenging impertinence. "Unaging monuments of intellect," perhaps even our brains, are covered with graffiti. At whose entrance do students rise? *Plus de Maîtres* proclaimed one of the passwords blooming on the walls of the Sorbonne in May 1968.

Scientism; feminism; mass democracy and its media. Can, should "the lessons of the Masters" survive their tidal onrush?

I believe that they will, even if it is in unforseeable guise. I believe that they must. *Libido sciendi,* a lust for knowledge, an ache for understanding is incised in the best of men and women. As is the calling of the teacher. There is no craft more privileged. To awaken in another human being powers, dreams beyond one's own; to induce in others a love for that which one loves; to make of one's inward present their future: this is a threefold adventure like no other. As its spreads, the family of one's sometime students is like the branching, the green of a trunk itself aging (I have students on five continents). It is a satisfaction beyond compare to be the servant, the courier of the essential—knowing perfectly well how very few can be creators or discoverers of the first rank. Even at a humble level—that of the schoolmaster—to teach, to teach well, is to be accomplice to transcendent possibility. Woken, that exasperating child in the back row may write the lines, may conjecture the theorem that will busy centuries. A society, such as that of unbridled profit, which does not honour its teachers, is flawed. It could be that this is the radical meaning of child pornography. Where men and women toil barefoot to seek out a Master (a frequent hasidic trope), the life force of the spirit is safeguarded.

We have seen that Mastery is fallible, that jealousy, vanity, falsehood, and betrayal intrude almost unavoidably. But its ever renewed hopes, the imperfect marvel of the thing, direct us to the *dignitas* in the human person, to its homecoming to its better self. No mechanical means, however expeditious, no materialism, however triumphant, can eradicate the daybreak we experience when we have understood a Master. That joy does nothing to alleviate death. But it makes one rage at its waste. Is there no time for another lesson?

Argument should end in poetry. No one has thought more deeply about the issues I have tried to raise than did Nietzsche:

> Oh Mensch! Gib Acht!
> Was spricht die tiefe Mitternacht?

"Ich schlief, ich schlief—,
"Aus tiefem Traum bin ich erwacht:—
"Die Welt ist tief,
"Und tiefer als der Tag gedacht,
"Tief ist ihr Weh—,
"Lust—tiefer noch als Herzeleid:
"Weh sprich: Vergeh!
"Doch alle Lust will Ewigkeit—,
"—will tiefe, tiefe, Ewigkeit!"

O mankind! Take guard!
What says deep midnight?
"I slept, I slept—,
"I have woken from a deep dream:—
"The world is deep,
"And deeper than thought the day.
"Its pain is deep—,
"Desire—deeper still than pain of heart:
"Grief says: go hence!
"But all lust seeks eternity—,
"—seeks deep, deep eternity!"

A halting attempt at translation. When there is already a soaring one: in Mahler's setting. Master to Master.

INDEX

◇ ◇ ◇